The Nature and Measurement of Competency in English

The project which led to this publication, *The Nature and Measurement of Competency in English*, was supported by grants from the NCTE Research Foundation established in honor of J. N. Hook and the Carnegie Corporation of New York.

The Nature and Measurement of Competency in English

Edited by

Charles R. Cooper
University of California, San Diego

National Council of Teachers of English
1111 Kenyon Road, Urbana, Illinois 61801

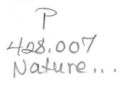

Book Design: Tom Kovacs

NCTE Stock Number 32626

Library of Congress Cataloging in Publication Data
Main entry under title:

The Nature and measurement of competency in English.

    Bibliography: p.
    1. English language—Study and teaching—Addresses, essays, lectures. 2. Competency based education—Addresses, essays, lectures. I. Cooper, Charles Raymond, 1934- . II. National Council of Teachers of English.
LB1576.N33   428'.007   81-11005
ISBN 0-8141-3262-6   AACR2

Contents

48016

Preface

State-mandated minimal competency testing or proficiency testing programs have appeared with dizzying speed in the last few years. Though the accountability movement in education began gathering momentum about twenty years ago, it had not produced centralized state-wide standards for promotion and graduation even as recently as 1974. Graduation requirements in nearly every state remained simply a certain number of course credits. Since 1974, however, every state in the country has adopted or is seriously considering an additional requirement of grade to grade promotion standards and high school graduation standards. What is now called in most places "minimal competency testing" will determine which students meet the standards. Observers of this development have used such language as "the most explosive issue on the educational scene today," "sweeping educational reform," or "striking development."

Elementary school reading and language arts teachers and secondary English teachers have a special stake in this momentous development: minimal competency testing is nearly always required in only the three areas of reading, writing, and math, and two of the three are in the domain of English.

Concerned about the implications of minimal competency testing for school English and reading programs, the Executive Committee of the National Council of Teachers of English (NCTE) in the spring of 1976 called for the formation of an ad hoc discussion group to explore this new development and to suggest various responses NCTE might make. This group met in September 1976 at NCTE headquarters in Urbana, Illinois. Present were Charles Cooper, Edmund J. Farrell, Allan Glatthorn, Jesse Perry, Alan Purves, and Gladys Veidemanis. One of several recommendations from this meeting was for a comprehensive, book-length response to the competency-testing movement, a book which would both provide a current statement of the nature of school English studies and offer some possibilities for the valid assessment of competencies or skills or performances in English. The statements about the nature of reading, writing, talking, listening, viewing were to reflect the best current theory, research, and practice and were to provide a context for a critique of early minimal competency tests and for suggestions about valid alternatives.

Charles Cooper agreed to assemble and chair a committee, Committee on English Competencies and Their Measurement, which would undertake this project. The following people agreed to serve on this committee:

Marilyn Hanf Buckley, University of California, Berkeley

Charles Cooper, Chair, University of California, San Diego

Allan Glatthorn, University of Pennsylvania

Mary Jane Hanson, Harrison School, Minneapolis, Minnesota

Herb Karl, University of South Florida

John Mellon, University of Illinois at Chicago Circle

Miles Myers, University of California, Berkeley

Lee Odell, Rensselaer Polytechnic Institute

Alan Purves, University of Illinois at Urbana-Champaign

Robert Quakenbush, Skiles Experimental Middle School, Evanston, Illinois

With temporary support from the Research Foundation of NCTE, we met for the first time at the November 1976 NCTE Convention in Chicago and discussed how we might carry out our charge. Herb Karl, John Mellon, Miles Myers, Lee Odell, and Alan Purves agreed to write chapters for the book and Charles Cooper took on the tasks of coordinating the project, editing the book, and contributing a chapter which would provide an overview of the competency-testing movement and survey issues in competency testing.

The whole committee met in Urbana in February 1977 to make more detailed plans for the book, and then the writers met in Chicago in June to discuss first drafts of their chapters. By this time Charles Cooper had written on behalf of the NCTE Executive Committee a proposal to the Carnegie Corporation of New York, requesting support for the project. The Carnegie Corporation agreed to support the project, and the committee is most grateful to Fritz Mosher, Carnegie program officer, for his interest in our project and support of the proposal.

During the next year the chapters were drafted and redrafted as they were circulated among all the members of the committee for comment, and the finished manuscript was submitted to the NCTE Editorial Board.

In the book we have tried to answer three major questions:

1. What is competence in English?

Answering this question led us into brief but comprehensive reviews of the best current theory, research, and practice in English education. Even though the motive for the book came from the current movement toward state-mandated minimal competency testing, we wanted to have a clear view of general competence before we talked about its minimal forms. Stating this first question led us to other questions which are basic to the work of English teachers:

> What do we know when we know a language?
>
> Exactly what does it mean to say that someone is a skilled or fluent or competent user of language?
>
> What is involved in the reading process?
>
> What skills does a fluent, practiced adult reader have?
>
> What is the nature of written discourse? How varied is it? Does this variety present problems for writers?
>
> How does the composing process work? What is actually involved in producing effective writing? What kinds of plans and decisions do writers make?

And then including media study in our broad definition of school English studies:

> Is it possible to talk about media competency? What might be involved in such competency?
>
> How can viewers of TV and movies learn what effects these nonprint media have? How is the effect of the medium itself different from the effect of its content?

We believed that answers to these questions were essential background for considering any questions about assessment or measurement. Still seeking background and context, we also tried to answer this major question:

2. What do we know about assessment of competence in English?

We know a great deal, of course. There have been decades of psychometric work in reading and language. The last few years have seen promising new work on the evaluation of writing. And yet this work had produced no widespread consensus about assessment. Indeed, as we were writing our chapters the National Education Association was intensifying its campaign to have all standardized tests banished from the schools. Reading tests have come under substantial theoretical and empirical challenge by reading researchers themselves. Writing specialists still argue over whether a multiple-choice standardized test has any place at all in evaluating writing performance.

And yet despite this lack of consensus, we believed we could usefully point readers to some of the most promising new developments in assessing competence in reading, writing, and media, and we knew we wanted to discuss some of the important current issues of assessment.

With the best current information in hand on the nature of school English studies and their assessment—or to say it more simply, with a good description of what the best-informed English teachers do in their classroom and how they evaluate the results— we felt more confident in approaching the third major question:

3. How can we define and assess minimal competency in English?

And, of course, this was the most problematic question. The first issue was whether a reasonable definition of *minimal* competency looked any different from a definition of *general* competency. How much is a little bit (a minimal amount) of competency for a writer and reader and watcher of TV advertising? Is that little bit the same amount for a nine year old, a thirteen year old, and a seventeen year old? The second issue was whether a *test* of this minimal competence would look any different from tests of general competency already widely in use in the schools. Did the minimal competency-testing movement require a new testing technology?

A third issue pervading all of our discussions and drafts and revisions was the differential effects on test-design and procedures and on school programs of *local* and *centralized* minimal competency testing. Though such testing is state-mandated, that is, enacted into law by a state legislature or decreed by a state school board or state education department, tests themselves can either be developed by individual schools or school districts or by central state education department special staffs: the state-mandated program in Oregon leaves competency definitions and test development to local schools and school boards; whereas in New York it is done by the state education department with the advice of committees of teachers, parents, and specialists, and the same competency tests are given statewide on specified dates. It seemed to us that local development held out the possibility of integrating competency testing (both minimal and general) with the instructional program, but that centralized statewide testing precluded that possibility. This issue seemed especially urgent in the case of writing assessment. On the other hand, only statewide testing enables a statewide standard to be enforced, assuming in the case of non-standardizable performance tests like writing that reliable, comparable scores can be achieved among all the school districts in the state.

These and many other issues about minimal competency testing reviewed in chapter 1 presented serious obstacles to us throughout the development of the book. With minimal competency testing viewed as a special and highly problematical case of general competency testing, individual authors have made whatever recommendations about minimal competency testing seemed reasonable to them considering the skill to be tested. Since so much remains unresolved about minimal competency testing, this book cannot be regarded as a complete handbook on the subject. Though writers make specific recommendations or outline various alternatives, they cannot offer complete programs.

Nor do all authors deal with the three major questions above in just the same way. Given the complexities of the various domains of school English studies, the committee at the outset proposed that the book be authored by specialists in each domain. Consequently, the book lacks the evenness of a textbook or monograph. These specialists speak in their own voices and offer their own individual insights, based on their wide experience and reading. What unites these chapters is the urgency the authors feel about the nature of school English studies and assessment in view of the surprising recent developments in state-mandated minimal competency testing.

We should also point out that the views of the committee and the individual authors are not necessarily the views of the NCTE Executive Committee or the Carnegie Corporation.

A brief overview here of each chapter will help the reader anticipate the organization of the book and the relationships among the chapters.

In chapter 1 Charles Cooper proposes an account of the origins and development of the competency-testing movement. He also discusses several major issues in the movement.

The readers should regard chapter 2 as the centerpiece of the book. In it John Mellon provides a comprehensive review of the best current research and theory on language—its acquisition and development and use. Since language is at the center of school

English studies, any consideration of teaching or testing must, we believe, be grounded in sound information about language and the ways humans use it. John Mellon makes an important distinction which initially may seem to be a somewhat distracting reversal of key terms in this book. Following the current distinction among linguists between competence and performance, he defines competence as innate, invariant ability and performance as the variable use of that ability in different language situations across the whole life-span. Clearly, with this distinction it is performance we test with a competency test, not innate competence. The linguist's distinction is a crucial one for Mellon's chapter, but in the remainder of the book and in our book title we are following the general use of "competency" to mean performance.

With chapter 2 as background, chapters 3 and 4 take up the two domains in English of critical importance in the current competency-testing movement: reading and writing. In chapter 3, Alan Purves examines the limitations of various approaches to testing reading ability and then proposes a four-part competency test made up of some of the best available test formats. In chapter 4, Lee Odell outlines in detail a theory-based procedure for assessing writing competence. Neither writer offers a specific minimal competency test, but both offer a rich context of issues and possibilities for those who will be constructing such tests.

In chapter 5, Herb Karl explores the problems of assessing media competency. Though no state we are aware of is planning to assess media competency and though few schools give media studies a prominent place in their programs, the committee and all the authors believe this chapter is important. A major issue in competency testing is whether the narrow concern with testing reading and writing will produce equally narrow English programs. We were most concerned that the book reflect our own broad view of school English studies, which certainly includes media studies. Herb Karl does not propose a minimal competency-testing program for the good reason that almost no one in media studies has given much attention yet to general competency testing.

The book concludes with a chapter Miles Myers calls a "political postscript." Part of the response English teachers could make to the competency-testing movement is to deepen their research and scholarship and to revitalize their remedial teaching, but another part of their response must be political, we believe. To pretend that the movement is not intensely political, at least at the state level, is to be naive. Where teachers or parents wish to change legislation mandating competency-testing programs, they will need to enter the political process and do it in a sophisticated and organized way.

Though Myers doesn't discuss it, there is a special form of *educational* politics English teachers must be sensitive to: educational theorists and researchers and curriculum specialists slight or ignore the basic questions about competency testing in language, reading, writing, and media. To choose from among recent examples, two major books on competency testing have appeared, *Minimum Competency Achievement Testing: Motives, Models, Measures, and Consequences* (Richard M. Jaeger and Carol Kehr Tittle, editors. Berkeley: McCutchan, 1980) and *Minimal Competency Testing* (Peter E. Airasian, George F. Madaus, and Joseph J. Pedulla, editors. Englewood Cliffs, N.J.: Educational Technology Publications, 1979), and both of them are innocent of the crucial learning and measurement issues explored in chapters 2–5 of this book. An English teacher—or a parent, school administrator, or school board member—reading these books gets the impression that the issues in minimal competency testing are solely historical, legal, social, administrative, psychometric, public relational, and general curricular. There is barely a hint that English programs specifically are the most threatened by the competency-testing movement or that valid competency testing and effective competency teaching will simply fail unless they are based on the best current understanding we can reach about the nature of language development, reading, and writing.

Of course, the issues addressed in these two books are important. The books are useful and should be widely read, especially by English teachers. But there is much, much more to be said about the competency-testing movement; and English teachers in schools and colleges will have to say it. We believe this book will be a starting point for English teachers and for anyone else concerned about the future of school and college English studies.

We have written the book for a wide audience:

> teachers, administrators, and local school board members responsible for implementing state-mandated competency-testing programs
>
> state and national assessors and test publishers who are developing competency-testing programs
>
> research and evaluation specialists, as well as classroom teachers, interested in pursuing measurement issues in English studies within the context of the best current definition of those studies

teachers and teachers-in-training who are curious about the
impact of recent research and theory on the definition of
English studies

Even though much of the book is about measurement, we have
avoided technical jargon. Furthermore, we have assumed that
many of our readers will not have backgrounds in English education. We intend our book to be engaging for the nonspecialist.

Charles R. Cooper

1 Competency Testing: Issues and Overview

Charles R. Cooper
University of California, San Diego

This book is about the nature and assessment of competence in English. It appears at a time when there is widespread concern about minimal competence or basic skills, at a time when minimal competency testing is being considered or has already been legislated in every state in the nation. Language from a 1976 California law succinctly reflects that concern:

> The Legislature finds that high school graduation requirements are generally related to "seat time" and tied to college entrance requirements. The Legislature further finds that pupils currently graduating from the public schools may lack competence in essential communication and computation skills, and the confidence that they can cope successfully with a complex, contemporary society.
>
> It is the intent and purpose of the Legislature, by the provisions of this act, to ensure the development of clearly defined proficiency standards in communication and computation skills for pupils graduating from public secondary schools. It is the purpose of this act to ensure early identification of pupils lacking competence in basic communication and computation skills, so that such pupils can be provided with repeated opportunities to achieve prescribed standards of proficiency.

Why have state legislatures and state school boards in California and many other states adopted this way of talking about public schooling? What are the implications of state-mandated minimal competency testing for elementary and secondary school English language arts programs? What are the basic issues in competency testing?

Definition of Competency Testing

Before we take up these questions, it would be convenient to have a simple definition of competency testing. We can devise one; but

1

it will have to be somewhat arbitrary, given the conceptual and terminological confusion accompanying the call for minimal competency standards. The idea has its origins in the accountability movement, which took its principles from an industrial management approach emphasizing output and measures of output. Adapted to education, this movement has produced over the last fifteen years a number of newly-labeled activities: (1) competency-based education (CBE), (2) performance-based education (PBE), (3) competency-based teacher education (CBTE), (4) competency-based teacher certification (CBTC), (5) assessment systems (federal, state and local), (6) program evaluation, (7) learner verification, (8) behavioral objectives, (9) mastery learning, (10) criterion-referenced testing, (11) educational indicators, and (12) performance contracting (Wise, 1977).

A little reading in the literature on competency testing turns up this range of terms: capacities, enabling capacities, enriching capacities, proficiencies, competencies, minimal competencies, basic competencies, enabling competencies, life role competencies, survival skills, baseline skills, and functional literacy. The reader can find testing itself referred to in the following ways: minimal competency testing, applied performance testing, or measuring basic life skills. But the most common terms seem to be *competency* and *competency testing*. The complex issues we will discuss in a moment notwithstanding, we can say for now that *competency testing is a procedure for determining what a student knows or can do relative to some standard of performance.* The testing does not compare students to each other, but rather establishes whether they meet a certain standard. Most present tests are tests of "minimal" competence and purport to concern themselves only with reading, writing, and math. Some test only what is learned in school; others test what is presumably required of an efficient worker, careful consumer, or good citizen. Here are examples of some of the first competency tests:

> *Example 1*: The New York State "Basic Competency Test in Writing Skills" (October 1976) given in Grade 9 has the following format:
>
> > Part 1: Spelling: ten words dictated by the teacher
> > Part 2: Mechanics: ten multiple choice items
> > Part 3: Sentence Writing: ten phrases to use in writing out ten sentences
> > Part 4: Paragraph: a request to write a paragraph of five sentences on what you would say at a community meeting called to make rules to control dogs

Part 5: Letter: a request to write a letter ordering a poster set from an advertisement

Note: This test was phased out in 1980 and replaced with a new test requiring three writing samples. The new test is titled "New York State Competency Test in Writing."

Example 2: The Philadelphia schools test, "The Assessment of Functional Literacy in High School," given in Grade 12, is organized like this:

Part A: Vocabulary: thirty multiple-choice items

Part B: Reading: fifty multiple-choice items based on selections from newspapers, magazines, and job-connected materials

Part C: Job Application: request to fill out a form requiring about ten separate pieces of personal information

Example 3: The California Test Bureau of McGraw-Hill publishes a series of tests called *Proficiency and Review*. For high school students Test III is titled Language Proficiency. Test IV is titled Reading Proficiency. The directions to the student announce, "These are tests designed to measure your ability in certain basic skills, which you have been developing since you first started school." The tests are organized as follows:

Language Proficiency
Punctuation, capitalization, grammar: fifty items in a multiple-choice proofreading format. The student searches for errors in two short paragraphs.

Reading Proficiency
Reading comprehension: three short reading selections with eight statements about each selection. The student decides whether the statement is in agreement or disagreement with the selection or is "neither stated nor suggested" in the selection.

Vocabulary: twenty-five multiple-choice synonym items.

Example 4: In September of 1977 Educational Testing Service made available to schools its Basic Skills Assessment Program for math, reading, and writing. The reading and writing exams have the following formats:

Reading: sixty-five multiple-choice items based on selections in five categories: consumer, learner, citizen, protector, and producer. Examples of selections are job application, bus schedule, want ad, medicine label, road map, tax form, newspaper editorial, school catalog, book-titles, narrative fiction, loan agreement, telephone directory.

Writing: sixty multiple-choice items, mainly mechanics and usage. There is also a writing *option* where students may be asked to do the following: organize and express thoughts about a visual or written stimulus, accurately convey information provided in a test booklet or on a tape recording, or fill out a simple application form.

Of the foregoing examples, one test was produced by a state education department, one by an urban school district central office staff, and the other two by large test manufacturers. The main impression these representative tests give is one of conventionality. At the least the competency-testing movement does not yet seem to be producing a test technology any different from our present one. When reviewing these tests closely from my perspective as a high school English teacher for nine years, as a parent of a child in junior high school, and now as a testing and evaluation specialist, I felt uncertain whether to be relieved (This will be an easy mark!) or alarmed (Are assessment specialists seriously going to ask us to use these?) or cynical (Ah, I see. No one is taking this seriously, not even assessment specialists.) or despairing (Is this what parents worried about basic skills are willing to settle for? or Well, it must be a political move to keep minorities in their place after all.) I feel certain many English language arts and reading teachers, parents, and school board members will have similar reactions.

In addition to their conventionality, we can note that nearly all these examples have too few items or too few selections in each section of the test to be reliable. Furthermore, even if the tests were valid and even if they did reliably separate the competent from the not competent, they would give us no information about what kinds of help the noncompetent will need. We can also wonder about the popularity of vocabulary subtests. They have a certain acceptability as a predictor of reading ability, but one can only be puzzled about their use in achievement or competency tests.

We can only guess what an acceptable standard of performance might be on these tests, although we can presume that scoring manuals accompanying the test might offer some guidelines. What kind of standard would be realistic in Grade 9? Twenty of thirty vocabulary items? Eight of ten spelling items? Ordinarily, performance standards would be established after extensive tryouts, but we know this was not done with the Functional Literacy Test used statewide in Florida in October 1977 (Glass, 1978). One good thing to be said for these four examples is that one of them asks the student to produce actual writing. We might also note that in two of them the reading selections seem quite varied, though they are very brief.

But a complete analysis of these examples is not appropriate here. That's what the whole book is about. I offer them here mainly to help us reach an understanding of the competency-testing movement. We can say, in summary, that competency tests are designed to identify students who fail to meet a certain standard. Unique to these tests is the requirement that they enable us to make a two-way decision: this student is competent (or minimally competent) or not competent. The tests themselves should be valid for particular competency-based education programs (more about them later). In fact, though, state education departments and state legislatures have decided to mandate the tests only, rather than the instructional programs that underlie them. The assumption seems to be that the mandated competency tests will force the schools to develop competency-based educational programs. (I can't resist pointing out the irony of state and federal educational agencies insisting on a particular form of testing in the context of the management by objectives movement, which has always had as its basic principle that clear statements of objectives and a careful description of instructional programs to achieve the objectives should *precede* test design.)

We have seen that many presently available competency tests seem narrow and conventional. And this is exactly the issue: since only the tests are being mandated, and since the tests are narrow and invalid from the perspective of the best current definition English teachers have of their field, then the tests are likely to result in narrowly conceived and ineffective instruction.

Some Causes of the Competency-Testing Movement

There are a number of reasons why the competency-testing movement is gaining so much momentum at just this time. Quite clearly the general public and state legislators believe the schools are failing to do their job. There is evidence from the U.S. Office of Education that about twenty-three million Americans lack basic literacy skills. *Newsweek* (20 April 1981) reports a Gallup Poll that shows 59 percent of adults surveyed believe "teachers should be better trained; more than 60 percent want their children taught in a more orderly atmosphere; almost 70 percent call for more stress on the academic Basics." There seems little argument even from school people that the schools could do better.

And yet teachers have been rightfully irritated by recent attacks from the media. The evidence that schools are doing a worse job than they were ten years ago or fifty years ago is quite inconclusive. The most reliable data come from the surveys of the National Assessment of Educational Progress (NAEP), and those data indicate a slight downturn in writing, science, and math achievement over the last ten years but an upturn in reading. However, these general trends obscure evidence of improved achievement at certain age levels and in certain kinds of skills. For example, in science, achievement in biology is up for nine and thirteen year olds, but down in physical science for those ages. In writing, there is a very slight decline in overall writing ability (what John Mellon in chapter 2 calls discourse skills), but no decline in the basic skills of writing: spelling, punctuation, capitalization, usage. In math, all of the decline is in general problem solving ability, not in the basic computational skills of adding and subtracting and multiplying. Consequently, we can say that the best data available—those derived from a nation-wide testing program designed specifically to monitor changes in achievement—show some improvements and some declines and probably on average, all the results taken together, a very slight decline. It is interesting to note that achievement over ten years in the basic skills of writing mechanics and math computation—the main concern of competency-testing advocates—has been stable, while the higher cognitive skills of composing and problem solving have declined. This result suggests that the problem may not be where some think it is: with the minimal skills of bare functional literacy; rather, the problem seems to be with the maximal skills of thinking, creating, and problem-solving.

Of most concern to the media have been falling scores on the Scholastic Aptitude Test (SAT), a college entrance exam taken by well over a million high school seniors each year. From 1963 to 1980 the scores on the verbal section of the SAT dropped from 478 to 424 (down 54 points), while the scores on the math section dropped from 502 to 466 (down 36 points). A 1977 report of a comprehensive study of these score declines concluded that most of the decline between 1963 and 1970 could be explained by the fact that a more diverse group of students was taking the test and planning to go on to college but that most of the change after 1970 could be explained by six factors: changes in the school curriculum, low standards in schools, television, broken families, social and political disruption, and low motivation (*On Further Examination*). Clearly, a good part of the blame is being placed on the schools (two of the six reasons and possibly a third, motivation). Yet the report notes the NAEP results I mentioned above and points out as well that NAEP's test in Functional Literacy and Basic Reading Performance shows an increase in reading performance between 1969 and 1973. Still other evidence of improvement in reading performance comes from tests given to army inductees from World

War II to the present. The report also points out that over the period of the SAT score decline, scores on College Entrance Examination Board Achievement Tests have declined only slightly on four tests but *increased* on six others (writing, three foreign languages, chemistry, physics). How are we to explain this curious result: decline in SAT scores, but increases in achievement test scores? Why has the College Entrance Examination Board not convened a prestigious national panel to seek explanations for *increases* in achievement of high school graduates? As this score decline controversy swirls around us, we need to keep in mind that the SAT is an aptitude, not an achievement, test. Its purpose is to predict grades earned in college. It is a combination of vocabulary and reading comprehension items (I have already noted the uselessness of vocabulary items on achievement or competence tests). We also need to remember that the SAT Verbal is not a writing test.

Despite the evidence for improved achievement I have just cited, the general public believes there is a lack of standards in the schools and that the high school diploma no longer has any meaning. They believe it so strongly that in one Gallup Poll 65 percent of adults polled favored a *nation-wide* high school graduation test as a way to improve standards in the schools. This belief in falling standards is regularly encouraged by news stories like those about Stephen Jackson and Edward Donohue. Stephen Jackson was the valedictorian of his 1976 class at the District of Columbia's Western High School, and yet his SAT verbal score was only 320 and his math score 280, placing him in the bottom 13 percent and 2 percent respectively of those college-bound students who take the SAT. George Washington University, Jackson's first choice, declined to admit him; he was accepted at the University of Pittsburgh, Boston University, and Howard University, but with certain conditions at all three. He chose Howard University, where he was asked to prove himself in the liberal arts curriculum before studying accounting.

Edward Donohue and his parents sued the Copiague (New York) Union Free Schools for five million dollars on the grounds of "educational malpractice." (They lost the much-publicized suit.) Donohue graduated from high school unable to read, but was learning with the aid of a private tutor. One of the allegations in the legal action was that his school failed to administer tests that would have indicated why he was doing so poorly and how he might be helped. Donohue's mother said that over the years she had asked the schools about her son's poor grades but was told repeatedly that he was getting sufficient help and that he would improve.

Some teachers blamed Donohue's lack of achievement on his attitude toward school, noting that he was suspended twice in Grade 8 for fighting and that his attendance record was not good.

Donohue's English courses and grades made an unusual pattern (65 is a passing grade):

    Grade 9: English 1, 70
    Grade 10: English 1C, 58
    Grade 11: English 2C, 50
    Grade 12: English 3C, 65
              English 4, 68
              English 2, (Independent Study) 65

Passing the three English courses in Grade 12 enabled him to graduate and receive his diploma. He argued that this unusual senior year program was designed to push him out of the school. He said, "When I realized that they were going to pass me anyway, I didn't do any more work" (*New York Times*, 20 February 1977, p. 56).

Besides the suspicion of failure and lack of standards, many people feel hostility toward teachers, who now regularly go on strike to improve salaries or working conditions. There has been much stress lately on holding teachers "accountable." No doubt the current large over-supply of teachers has encouraged school boards to highlight the accountability issue. Many parents are uneasy about experimental teaching and new programs and are hoping for a return to the "basics." In the yearly Gallup Poll of attitudes toward education "lack of discipline" has been the *major* concern of the public in nearly every one of the polls over the last eight or nine years.

News from the big cities encourages people's suspicions that the schools are failing. I think it is fair to say that there is considerable despair about schools, particularly secondary schools, in nearly every big city. Attendance is poor, the drop-out rate is high, vandalism and personal attacks on students and teachers are not unusual. Teachers are discouraged. Students are disaffected. Parents are resentful. Moreover, businessmen and industrialists insist that young employees lack basic skills. These are facts to be confirmed in our cities; I mention them only as one further reason why many people believe the schools are failing to do their job.

Public clamor and judgments about its validity aside, there have been important recent activities within education which have prepared the way for competency testing. We have seen the development of a major new form of testing—objectives-based or criterion-referenced testing—which has challenged norm-referenced or standardized testing. These new tests tell us what a particular student can or cannot do, what specific instructional objectives a student has achieved, rather than merely telling us how the student stands relative to other students on the test, as is the case with a norm-referenced test. Another version of this new form of testing is called domain-referenced testing. In this version a domain of knowledge is identified and test items are constructed to sample the entire domain. The results tell us how much of the domain the student knows. Nearly all of the recently-mandated competency-testing programs use domain-referenced or criterion-referenced tests. Since the best of these tests given under the best of conditions do permit us to collect information about a student's proficiency or competency, they have given a certain respectability to the competency-testing movement. The National Assessment of Educational Progress uses criterion-referenced tests and has been instrumental in popularizing their use by state education departments (English teachers will want to know John Mellon's insightful critique, *National Assessment and the Teaching of English*, 1975). Consequently, since the late 1960s large pools of test items have been developed in many states and these have been drawn on for some of the early competency tests.

I should point out that National Assessment and various state assessments are designed to determine levels of achievement of large groups (schools, school districts, or large regions of the country) and to monitor group changes in achievement over time. To achieve this purpose such assessments need to test only small samples of students in a particular school or region. What is of interest is performance on an item in the test by a sample of students, not the performance on all the items by each individual student. By contrast, state-mandated competency tests are designed to determine whether each individual student is writing or reading or computing "adequately."

Another educational development that has prepared the way for competency testing is mastery learning, a new model of instruction which has attracted increasing attention in the last few years (Block, 1974; Bloom, 1971; Carroll, 1963). Its basic assumption is quite simple: nearly anyone can learn most of what we teach in schools, given reasonable interest in learning, good instruction, and enough time to learn. Mastery learning requires explicit statements about what the student is to learn—statements which are shared with the student—and regular assessment of how well the student is progressing toward the stated instructional objectives. Mastery learning also assumes that since students have different learning styles, as well as different learning rates, instructional materials and teaching approaches must be quite varied and appropriate to the student and the task. Actually, it is more accurate to say that this model of instruction is *revived*, not *new*. In 1926 Morrison advocated a very similar approach with his *mastery unit*. It involved specific statements of objectives, varied tasks and materials, and no moving on until mastery was obtained (Applebee, 1974).

English teachers around the country first made their acquaintance with mastery learning and related matters such as behavioral objectives when asked during the late 1960s to write behavioral (or performance or instructional) objectives for their courses. Within the English teaching profession this became a major issue. It was addressed in a series of publications sponsored by the National Council of Teachers of English (see the appendix to this chapter) and catalogs of objectives for English instruction became available (Hook, *et al.*, 1971). English teachers also struggled with the serious testing issues raised by the use of behavioral objectives, issues which were never resolved satisfactorily and which continue with the competency-testing movement. In chapter 2 of this book John Mellon addresses the dangers to the English curriculum of teaching and testing skills piecemeal.

English teachers who know the history of their subject must be thinking often these days about the cult of efficiency which became prominent in the 1920s. Then, as now, there was an intense concern with practical outcomes, with minimal essentials and basic skills, and with testing. There was a great deal of talk at all levels in the profession about scientific management and about objective testing, which had just become widespread and had fostered a new science, psychometrics. Curiously, both conservative and liberal English teachers rallied behind the objective-testing movement, conservatives because it enforced standards and discipline, liberals because it enabled them to diagnose students' learning problems and correct them. Surveying these developments Arthur Applebee (1974, p. 81) concludes: "the response to the pressures for efficiency was too extreme, carrying with it the seeds of damage to the teaching profession as a whole. In many school systems, 'efficient' education came to be identified too closely with 'good' education, and broader perspectives to be submerged in the concern with budgets and short-term 'results'."

Reminding ourselves about the cult of efficiency (Callahan, 1962) might make us wonder whether there is anything new in the competency-testing movement, whether we're just seeing a repeat of the 1920s. Complex political, economic, and social pressures may force us occasionally into one of these bouts of efficiency and accountability. The schools have always been vulnerable to certain national anxieties.

So far I've been able to point to certain public perceptions and to recent educational developments lying behind the competency-testing movement. Recent evaluators of the movement have pointed out still other sources. When the schools failed to insure equal education opportunity, parents went beyond local schools to higher authorities and to the courts. In recent years the courts have also had to intervene to insure equal treatment for women teachers and administrators, equal resources for women's athletic programs, access by parents to their children's school records, full educational benefits for the handicapped, protection of teachers from arbitrary dismissal, and guarantees that students could not be suspended without a hearing. Since local school officials were unable to resolve these significant issues of educational policy, the result has been a diminution of local authority and an increasing centralization of school governance (Wise, 1977). Such centralization has eased the acceptance of state-mandated promotion and graduation standards and of centrally-prepared and centrally-administered competency tests.

We also need to remind ourselves that we have just emerged from a decade or more of energetic criticism of the schools by the so-called libertarian critics. Schools have been pictured as essentially damaging to the human spirit (Holt, 1964; Kohl, 1967; Herndon, 1971) and as places where teachers have little understanding of why they are doing what they are doing (Silberman, 1970). We have been told that we would be better off without schools in their present form (Illich, 1972). The competency-testing movement may be, in part, a corrective counter-balance to the liberal critique.

Other possible causes could be the current nostalgia for the past, for the good old days of spelling tests and McGuffey's readers, and the return to political and economic conservatism (Anderson, 1977). Still another cause might be high property and income taxes. It's not just that middle-class property owners prefer that no additional money be spent on education and that current money be used more efficiently, they also want their children to achieve well enough to be admitted to good colleges and eventually into graduate and professional programs. Since the real outcry is coming from the "overtaxed middle class parents of underachieving or less able children," the issue has come to involve "the politics of selection and opportunity" (Kelley, 1977). In chapter 6, Miles Myers explores this significant political issue.

Issues in the Competency-Testing Movement

Issues—confusions, questions, uncertainties—seem numberless in a controversial, rapidly-developing movement like competency-testing. For me and for many English teachers the main issue, the one subsuming all the rest, is the adverse effect on instruction of lowered expectations and of narrowly-conceived competency tests. I see the real likelihood of a dessicated English curriculum. This threat has a number of components, which I will discuss in turn.

The tail wags the dog. From the required reading lists of the College Entrance Examination Board at the turn of the century to the great variety of tests presently mandated by states and school districts it has been only too easy to document the reactive effect of testing on teaching. If teachers are to be held accountable primarily by the performance of their students on narrow basic skills tests, then instruction will inevitably be narrowed to objectives appropriate to the tests. If writing tests require no writing—and many we have seen do not—then writing instruction will be reduced to arhetorical drill on correct usage. If reading tests test only literal comprehension, then reading instruction will neglect or ignore inferential and critical reading skills.

Competency-based Education *as a context for competency-based* Testing. Behind the current obsession with competency testing is a teaching model which, were it put in place, would bring about a radical change in schooling (Mitchell and Spady, 1980). The nature of this radical change can be simply stated: graduation from high school would no longer be determined solely by number of courses and grades earned in courses. Graduation from high school would no longer require only so many semesters (or Carnegie units) of English, but would require instead or in addition demonstrated competence in the skills central to school English studies.

This new expectation of English programs would require a comprehensive approach to evaluation. We would be expected to describe or diagnose very precisely how well each student speaks and listens, writes, reads, and responds to literature and nonprint media. We would have to establish performance standards or criteria for each of these skills so that we could identify those students who do not perform well enough and would therefore need special help. We would be required to develop new ways to monitor the development of all students, particularly those who need special help. Finally, if we were to accept the assumptions of the currently-most-influential model of school learning (Carroll, 1963), we would have to assume that 95 percent of our students could acquire reasonable, literate levels of skill in English. This is a more revolutionary assumption than it appears. If we accept it, then *time spent developing the skill* takes precedence over time spent in courses of a certain duration. We would have to reconceive how we organize the English program and how we monitor students' progress through it. For example, a student who did not write well in Grade 9 would need sustained, personalized instruction in writing for so long as it took him or her to improve.

The problem is that while many state departments of education and school districts are presently rushing ahead with competency *testing*, they are not developing at the same time a comprehensive competency-based *education* program. Without such a program, competency testing creates more problems than it solves. Even in a good competency-based education program, like the one outlined just above, testing is the most troublesome feature. The question English teachers should be asking is whether administrators, local and state board members, and state legislators are interested in the comprehensive school reform called for in the competency-based education model—or some other model—or whether they are interested only in superficial testing programs. School reform costs money, especially when it leads to more attention to individual students.

Grade level of testing. For competency testing to be more than a procedure for differentiating diplomas at Grade 12, it will have to begin at least as early as Grade 9, and probably earlier. Students who lack competencies will need time to develop them. Furthermore, since we know from developmental psychology that students can do certain things at age seventeen they cannot do at age ten or even at age fourteen, we would anticipate different forms of the tests for different age levels.

Limitations of a competency test. Competency tests can identify students who fall short of a certain standard, but they cannot tell us what help the student needs. If we are going to insist on certain kinds of competency, then we must quickly develop comprehensive descriptive or diagnostic tests that will tell us precisely what a student can do and cannot do. The results of these tests will have to identify the kind of instruction a student needs. Competency tests *categorize* students. Diagnostic tests tell us *how to help* students. Teachers, administrators, and school board members will need to be particularly wary of test publishers claiming too much for their competency tests.

Remedial teaching to insure competence. No one really quarrels with the importance of identifying students who have not learned. But once we know who they are and have diagnosed their problems, we must be prepared to assist them with skillful remedial teaching. This approach makes a competence statement or objective something the school must do for the student, not a hurdle the student must leap. There is always the danger that competency testing will shunt certain numbers of students aside from the regular school and into intensive remedial instruction, isolating them from other students. This already happens in the tracking programs in many schools.

How are helpful and egalitarian remedial programs to be financed? How is the relatively stable teacher force to be trained to work in them? We need a great deal of research on remedial teaching, in the manner of Mina Shaughnessy's *Errors and Expectations* (1977). From the research we have and from our experience in the classroom, we know that remedial teaching in English requires a great deal of small group and individual work. We obviously need to know much more about tutoring programs (teacher-student, peer, cross-age), about small group processes in the classroom, and about self-help instructional programs.

Expectation level of competency statements. This might have been identified as the *minimal-maximal* issue. It raises a crucial question of whether competence statements and testing should be limited to basic survival skills, that is, to *minimal* competencies, or whether they should look more broadly at a range of competencies traditionally expected as the outcomes of twelve years of schooling. Why not test mathematics rather than arithmetic, why not test the full human use of language rather than spelling and editorial skills? Too low a level of competency statements can easily lead to reductionism in testing and curricula.

One critic of the competency-testing movement (Wise, 1977) has pointed out that an overemphasis on minimal competencies necessary to function as an adult "elevates to prime position the belief that the purpose of school is to prepare young people to take their place in society. In so doing, it creates an extremely functionist view of the relationship between the individual and society and the school's role in perpetuating the *status quo*. It emphasizes minimal education outcomes rather than 'equality of educational opportunity' or the 'maximal development of individual potential.' While these phrases also have a rhetorical component, they tend to lift our aspirations and expectations. . . . Minimal competency testing represents a narrowly instrumental view of the purpose of education." Still another critic (Broudy, 1980) has noted, "there has been a general agreement in rhetoric and sentiment that the public schools, envisioning universal attendance from grades K-12, would prepare us all for occupational, civic, and personal adequacy—that is, for being good citizens in a democratic, humane, high-achievement society. This agreement clearly committed the public schools to a curriculum that went well beyond the three R's for *all* children, especially when compulsory attendance was extended into early adolescence."

A higher level of competency statements, a broader but still realistic set of expectations for graduates, seems more in keeping with the goals of education in a democracy. All the authors in this book recommend such an approach.

Generic and specific statements of competence. Shall statements take the form of what adults need to do or of general skills that enable students to cope later with adult tasks? In my view the reactive effect on instruction will be quite negative if the adult skill or survival skill approach is used. In these tests students are required to show that they can do what adults in our society must do—fill out income tax forms or job applications and read instructions on paint cans or warnings on medicine labels. How shall we teach a student who performs poorly on such a test? The temptation seems nearly irresistible to have the student practice the reading of instructions or the filling in of forms. However, such practice prevents the student from acquiring the basic, underlying skills which would permit success with the more complex adult skill. Besides, what happens to the marginally literate student who has been trained to fill in a form a certain way when the form-makers change the directions? The IRS regularly changes its forms, as all of us adults know to our bafflement and dismay. The general skills approach, the one I favor, would lead us to test what is learned in school, rather than what is needed on the job.

Centralization of competency testing. Should a common test be constructed or purchased by a state or school district and then mandated for each school? In Oregon there is a general statewide statement of expectations for high school graduates, but testing is decentralized: school districts devise their own tests of whether students have met the statewide expectations. In New York testing is centralized: exams are constructed in Albany and mailed out to all school districts, where the tests must be administered on a particular day. Is statewide testing required in order to maintain standards between school districts? Doesn't centralized testing usually mean pencil-and-paper, machine-scorable tests? (It doesn't in New York or South Carolina.) On the other hand, do all local school districts have the expertise to design valid, comprehensive competency-testing programs? For English studies in particular what are the implications for local test development of the lack of information about new developments in the areas of language, rhetoric, discourse theory, the reading process, response to literature, and valid and varied testing formats? Can we assume that every teacher and administrator working on a competency test knows the basic facts about language which John Mellon outlines so comprehensively in chapter 2?

Nearly all English teachers would argue that certain competencies—even minimal ones—can be assessed only with some kind of demonstration or performance, not with a multiple-choice test. The administrative requirements of centralized testing too often preclude real performance tests of the kind Lee Odell advocates for writing in chapter 4.

Native language competency tests. Should a student arriving here at fifteen speaking only Portuguese be expected to pass competency tests at age seventeen in English? The California State Legislature says, "yes."

Conclusion

All of these issues remain central to the competency-testing movement. Their resolution in the years ahead will have a dramatic impact on language arts and English programs. We need to be particularly alert to insure that competency tests, whatever form they take, do not trivialize English programs. Most important, we need to make every effort to insure that competency tests are valid, that they reflect the best current definition of our subject and the most imaginative test formats or procedures we can devise.

To insure valid tests we are all going to have to be involved in the process by which competency tests are legislated, designed, critiqued, and redesigned. Any present legislation can be amended. Any current competency test can be revised.

Since most of the activity is at the state level—in state legislatures and their committees and in state education departments—English language arts teachers will need to be certain that through their state organizations they are able to influence legislation and policy. Every state has an affiliate organization of the National Council of Teachers of English already organized for such efforts.

The chapters that follow provide the information English teachers need to examine critically the competency-testing programs already in place in their states or school districts and to influence positively the redesign of these programs or the plans for new programs. Much is at stake for English teachers. Almost certainly the definition of English studies in American schools for many years will be determined by the direction the competency-testing movement takes.

References

Anderson, Barry D. "The Costs of Legislated Minimal Competency Testing." A paper prepared for a series of regional conferences on minimal competency testing sponsored by the National Institute of Education, September 1977.

Applebee, A. *Tradition and Reform in the Teaching of English.* Urbana, Ill.: NCTE, 1974.

Block, J. H., ed. *Schools, Society and Mastery Learning.* New York: Holt, Rinehart and Winston, 1974.

Bloom, B.; Hastings, J. T.; and Madaus, G. *Handbook on Formative and Summative Evaluation of Student Learning.* New York: McGraw-Hill, 1971.

Broudy, Harry S. "Impact of Minimal Competency Testing on Curriculum." In *Minimum Competency Achievement Testing: Motives, Models, Measures, and Consequences,* edited by Richard M. Jaeger and Carol Kehr Tittle, Berkeley, Calif.: McCutchan, 1980.

Callahan, Raymond. *Education and the Cult of Efficiency.* Chicago: University of Chicago Press, 1962.

Carroll, J. B. "A Model of School Learning." *Teachers College Record* 64 (1963):723-33.

Glass, G. "The Florida Test of 'Functional Literacy': A Postscript to 'Standards and Criteria'." CLAC-5. Publication of the Conference on Language Attitudes and Composition, Department of English, Portland State University, May 1978, pp. 2-9.

Herndon, James. *How to Survive in Your Native Land.* New York: Bantam, 1971.

Holt, John. *Why Children Fail.* New York: Delta, 1964.

Hook J. N., *et al. Representative Performance Objectives for High School English.* New York: Ronald, 1971.

Illich, Ivan. *Deschooling Society.* New York: Harper and Row, 1972.

Kelley, E. W. "The Politics of Proficiency." A paper prepared for a series of regional conferences on minimal competency testing sponsored by the National Institute of Education, September 1977.

Kohl, Herbert. *36 Children.* New York: New American Library, 1967.

Mellon, John. *National Assessment and the Teaching of English*. Urbana, Ill.:
NCTE, 1975.

Mitchell, Douglas E., and Spady, William G. "Organizational Contexts for Im-
plementing Outcome-Based Education." In *Minimum Competency Achievement Testing: Motives, Models, Measures, and Consequences*, edited by
Richard M. Jaeger and Carol Kehr Tittle, Berkeley, Calif.: McCutchan,
1980.

On Further Examination. New York: College Entrance Examination Board,
1977.

Shaughnessy, M. P. *Errors and Expectations*. New York: Oxford University
Press, 1977.

Silberman, Charles. *Crisis in the Classroom*. New York: Random House, 1970.

Wise, A. "A Critique of 'Minimal Competency Testing'." A paper prepared for
a series of regional conferences on minimal competency testing sponsored
by the National Institute of Education, September 1977.

Appendix

Since the beginnings of the teacher accountability movement in the late
1960s, the National Council of Teachers of English has sponsored a number
of responses to the movement, through resolutions at its annual conventions,
in conferences and journals, by activities of its various committees and commissions, and in book-length studies. English teachers interested in a fuller
context for the issues and concerns explored in the present book will want to
read these book-length collections of articles:

> Maxwell, John, and Jovatt, Anthony, eds. *On Writing Behavioral Objec-
> tives for English*. Champaign, Ill.: NCTE, 1970.
>
> Maloney, Henry B., ed. *Accountability and the Teaching of English*.
> Urbana, Ill.: NCTE, 1972.
>
> Maloney, Henry B., ed. *Goal Making for English Teaching*. Urbana, Ill.:
> NCTE, 1973.
>
> Purves, Alan C. *Common Sense and Testing in English*. Urbana, Ill.:
> NCTE, 1975.

The two resolutions below were passed at the 1977 annual meeting of
NCTE in New York City:

On Legislatively Mandated Competency-Based Testing

BACKGROUND: Responsible educators recognize the need for standards of
competence in the language arts at all levels. Unfortunately, much legislatively
mandated competency-based testing assumes that English language arts competencies can be defined, agreed upon by all those interested in education,
and tested. In practice, competency-based testing overlooks alternative ways
to determine students' growth and achievement. At this time few of the assumptions underlying competency-based education have been substantiated
in practice, theory, or research. Be it therefore

RESOLVED that NCTE oppose legislatively mandated competency-based testing until such time as it is determined to be socially and educationally beneficial;

RESOLVED that NCTE work with legislators and other policy makers to determine how language competence can be best assured;

RESOLVED that appropriate NCTE standing committees and commissions examine alternative ways of assuring competence while determining through practice, theory, and research if competency-based education is in the best interests of all members of the educational community.

On Excessive Focus on Sub-Skills

BACKGROUND: The national media have recently reported the promotion and retention policies instituted by school systems such as Chicago, Illinois; Greenville County, Virginia; and Indian River County, Florida. These policies are requiring the teaching and testing of isolated skills in reading and writing with little value placed on students' comprehensive ability to read and write. The sequencing of skills is either arbitrarily formulated or is dictated by the content of specific management systems or standardized achievement tests. There is no evidence to support the assumption that students who are successful on the tests of these isolated skills will automatically become competent in language use.

Furthermore, equating these arbitrarily chosen assessment measures with the "basics" represents a narrowing of the curriculum and produces classrooms in which drill and testing dominate.

The test scores from this restricted assessment of abilities then become the basis for decisions about student promotion. The same test scores are increasingly being used to measure teacher competence, resulting in decisions to hire or fire. Consequently, the same narrow sub-skill focus limits the development of language ability in students, controlling the language arts curriculum, dictating teaching styles, and imposing threats to teacher job security.

For economically advantaged students, the effect of these skill hierarchies can be narrowing and dehumanizing. For students whose economic, social, and cultural or linguistic backgrounds are divergent, the system imposes arbitrary, often insurmountable barriers to their language development and results in reinstituting the segregation of those students. Therefore be it

RESOLVED that NCTE condemn the transformation of the English Language Arts Curriculum from a holistic concern for language development to sequenced but isolated and often unrelated sets of reading and writing skills;

RESOLVED that NCTE oppose as educationally unsound the use of mandated performance assessments as criteria for promotion and/or graduation of students;

RESOLVED that NCTE oppose the use of narrow assessments of student skill as criteria for the hiring and firing of teachers;

RESOLVED that NCTE actively campaign against testing practices and programs which, masquerading as improved education for all children, actually result in the segregation and tracking of students, thus denying them equal educational opportunity.

2 Language Competence

John Mellon
University of Illinois at Chicago Circle

Functional literacy, survival skills, the basics. These are popular labels for things American parents want their children to learn, and expect our schools to teach. Also named as educational goals are grade-level reading ability, correct grammar, mature speaking and listening habits, a good vocabulary, knowledge of standard written English, a wide reading background, and the ability to see through jargon, propaganda, advertising, and other kinds of language trickery. Professional educators often list additional objectives, such as taste and appreciation in literary art, use of writing for self expression and to create meaning, and an introductory acquaintance with the subject matter of literature, rhetoric, grammar, and visual studies. Most of us, whether parents or educators, would agree that a student who achieves these goals and objectives has attained *language competence*.

Presumably, language competence is easily identifiable and readily taught. Traditionally we have assumed that every young person who studies hard and completes high school ought to exhibit at least minimally acceptable language competence. Still the fact is, many do not—an unfortunate situation all too apparent today. But perhaps this commonsense view of language competence is deceptive, even unreal? Do we not err in thinking that development of language skills is merely a matter of more drill and practice, more memorization, more time spent with the latest reading kit or grammar workbook? To answer these questions, we first need to know what psychologists and linguists have learned about the nature of language competence and methods of language teaching. Only then will we be prepared to decide what are the proper policies and practices our schools should follow.

When we think of *language competence* not in a theoretical way but in the practical terms of school, we generally have one or another of three activities in mind—defining it, testing it, or teaching it. Of these, I shall deal most with defining and teaching, least with testing. One reason for the scant attention to testing is that a test can measure only bits and pieces of anything as complex as language skill, and can never yield more than the diagnosis of any learning problem it uncovers. Only teaching can provide a remedy. Yet good teaching depends upon our knowledge about the whole of language competence and the skills associated with it—how we define them, how they are acquired, and how teachers may nurture and maximize their development.

Very often one finds discussions about language learning confused from the outset, because many people do not understand that linguists and psychologists use the term *language competence* in a more restricted way than do educators and laypersons. When linguists talk about language competence, they carefully point out that they are referring to universal properties of every human mind. In the linguist's sense, language competence is independent of which particular language a person learns in infancy—English, Russian, Chinese, whatever. Partly innate and partly taken from the environment in a mysterious process for which scholars lack even an agreed-upon name, language competence is acquired during the first three or four years of life, and is more or less the same for all persons regardless of differences in intelligence, culture, or environment. In short, every child in the world, except those afflicted by radical brain damage, already possesses language competence on the first day he or she sets foot in school.

Obviously, this is not what teachers and parents mean by the term. Young children beginning school have thousands and thousands of words yet to learn, along with the web of conceptual knowledge those words include, to say nothing of the myriad skills and strategies of mature language use, all of which come into play whenever we read, write, speak, listen, or think. The linguist grants all this, but insists that vocabulary learning and skills acquisition are matters of *performance*, a term roughly the opposite of *competence*.

So the linguist distinguishes between competence (unconscious, naturally developed language knowledge, acquired without variation by all children during the preschool years) and performance (language skills acquired throughout the school years, variably from student to student, according to factors in each student's learning environment). But the teacher's natural question is, why bother about competence? Shouldn't we limit our concerns exclusively to performance skills, skills that *are* teachable? The answer would be yes, were it not that a number of vitally important guide-lines for the teaching of performance skills arise from the linguist's view of competence, even though competence itself, by our defini-tion, is unteachable.

Accordingly, I have divided this chapter into two parts. The first illustrates in simple terms the linguist's meaning of *competence*, thereby laying groundwork for a discussion of the guidelines for teaching just mentioned. The second part surveys the broad area of *performance skills*, skills which are used in the familiar classroom activities of reading, writing, and talking. It discusses how and even whether these skills are directly teachable, and speculates about how we should deal with incompetence, that is, cases where stu-dents seem deficient in skills learning.

Part One: Language Competence as Defined by Linguists

To repeat, when linguists use the term *language competence*, they are not referring to observable instances of language use (reading a newspaper, writing a letter, chatting with friends), but rather to a complex network of unconscious knowledge within our minds, knowledge that informs those language uses, that makes them pos-sible. But what *is* this knowledge?

Aspects of Language Competence

Here let me just list the names of five aspects of language compe-tence that linguists have identified:

 word-order principles

 semantic relationships

 sentence-combining transformations

 lexical feature systems

 logical conjunctions

The next several paragraphs illustrate these five aspects. But the illustrations do not include linguistic formulations, nor am I trying to inflict a grammar lesson on anyone. Instead, I simply want to show that to know language is to know a great deal more than we *realize* we know.

Word-order principles. To begin, here are two possible sequences of words and word inflections (s, ing):

 1. the bird s are chirp ing
 2. s bird the ing chirp are

If we imagine these to represent spoken utterances, we agree at once that every English-speaking person above the age of four or five will recognize 1 as an appropriately formed sentence of the language, but 2 as strange, an oddity that one would neither say nor expect to hear. The reason 2 seems odd is that it violates certain *principles of word order* that are a part of our language competence. The word-order principle involved here is that articles and auxiliaries (the, are) precede rather than follow the nouns and verbs with which they occur, while noun and verb inflections (s, ing) follow their nouns and verbs. Obviously we do not have to depend on conscious knowledge of nouns, verbs, articles, auxiliaries, and inflections, or of the principle of word order just stated. Yet *all* utterances in English conform to these principles. It is as if we had these principles, these rules of language, simply programmed into our minds. And the fact of the matter is, we do. It is the sum total of this program, the whole list of these unconscious word-order principles, that the linguist calls language competence.

Semantic relationships. But language competence refers to more than just rules of word order. It also includes knowledge of what are called *semantic relationships*, relationships of meaning. Every word in the language, taken by itself, signifies certain things. But when we use a word in a sentence, with other words, each word enters into certain semantic relationships with the others that make the sentence mean more than just the "total" of the significations of its words taken individually. Here are some illustrations:

3. poisoned Tommy fish got the by
4. Tommy got poisoned by the fish
5. the fish got poisoned by Tommy

We see that 3 contains familiar words but makes no statement. This is because it establishes no semantic relationships. On the other hand, we do understand 4 as a statement, wherein "fish" is the cause of a result, "poisoning," which was done to a victim, "Tommy," through the action of some unexpressed agent. In 5, also a statement, we understand "Tommy" to be the agent of some action which resulted in "poisoning" being done to a victim, "fish." And it is more than just word order that establishes semantic relationships, since the meaings in 4 and 5 can be identically expressed by the following statements, where the words "Tommy" and "fish" are in reverse order relative to their positions in 4 and 5:

6. the fish poisoned Tommy
7. Tommy poisoned the fish

Nor is the difference merely a matter of grammatical function, as subject or object. In 6 "fish" is the cause of the poisoning but not the agent—someone (including Tommy himself) had to feed it to Tommy. In 7, however, "Tommy" is the agent of the poisoning but not the cause—that had to be a lethal chemical of some sort.

But enough discussion. The point is that words in even such short sentences as these enter into various semantic relationships with one another. Although we seldom learn the formal names for these relationships, they nonetheless govern our understanding of sentences, and are a fundamental part of everyone's language competence. We may *think* we understand sentences without all the rigamarole about agents, victims, causes, and so on, but the fact is, we do not. It's just that we are nowhere nearly aware of everything our minds actually know.

Sentence-combining transformations. A third aspect of our language competence is knowledge of *sentence-combining transformations.* These are unconscious operations by means of which we automatically combine the simplest statements possible in the language, which would sound ridiculous if uttered separately, into the complex but perfectly ordinary-sounding sentences of our actual speech and writing. For example, read this storytime dialogue between mother and child:

Mother: Once there was a gentleman.
Child: Yes?
Mother: He was honest.
Child: What did he do?
Mother: He took a lady for his second wife.
Child: What about her?
Mother: She was proud.
Child: And?
Mother: She was disagreeable.
Child: And?
Mother: She had two daughters.
Child: What were they like?
Mother: They were exactly like her.
Child: I'm confused. Tell me the whole thing again.
Mother: Once there was an honest gentleman who took for his second wife a proud and disagreeable lady who had two daughters exactly like herself.
Child: Oh, I know, that's the beginning of "Cinderella!"

Examining the last sentence (which does of course happen to be the opening sentence of "Cinderella") we see that it consists of the seven simple statements of the mother in the dialogue, combined into one sentence, structurally complex although perfectly normal-sounding. The meaning of this complex sentence exactly equals those of the seven simple ones, since it consists of *nothing more than* the seven combined into one. In the combining process the simple sentences are changed in form—transformed—in various ways, as can be seen. This is why linguists refer to the process as transformational sentence combining.

Sentence combining also comes into play in language comprehension, that is, in listening and reading. Suppose we read this sentence in the daily paper:

> The jurors who were deadlocked for three days in the baby-murder trial of a California doctor say they were torn by doubts over the meaning of brain death.

At some point in the unconscious process of comprehending this sentence, we apparently deconstruct it into its basic statements, like this:

> the jurors say something
> something deadlocked the jurors for three days
> someone tried a doctor for murder
> the doctor was from California
> someone murdered a baby
> the jurors doubted something
> these doubts tore the jurors
> death means something
> the brain dies

Thus the same sentence-combining transformations are used in understanding the ordinary sentences we encounter in reading and listening as are used in putting together the sentences we write and speak.

Lexical feature systems. Another component of our language competence, which facilitates our learning of new vocabulary, consists of systems of what linguists call *lexical features.* Consider the following, where the artificial word "plashion" stands for a real word heard for the first time by the second child:

> If Child One says: *Dad got some plashion today,*
> Child Two will never say: *What's a plashion?*

The reason Child Two will not say "*a* plashion" is that "some" in the first statement identifies the new word "plashion" as non-countable and mass. This means that although it may be abstract or concrete, it won't pluralize and doesn't occur with "a" or "an." It is attributes of meaning such as noncountable and mass that linguists call *lexical features*. In the above example, if "plashion" is later referred to as "stuff," or likened to known words for physical substances, Child Two will further identify it as concrete, that is, will assign the lexical feature "concrete" to the word. The process will continue until Child Two discovers the specific information that distinguishes this word from words naming other noncountable mass-concrete substances, and thus completes his or her acquisition of the word "plashion." Lexical feature systems, then, are unconscious frameworks into which our minds fit newly learned words, whether we learn them at age five or seventy-five.

Logical conjunctions. Yet another component of language competence is the group of connective words that linguists call *logical conjunctions*. Logical conjunctions establish semantic links between entire sentences. They include words like "but," "and," "however," "if ... then," "although," and many more. Using them correctly requires knowledge of the meaning of the particular conjunction and of the logical fit between the sentences it joins. Oddities immediately call attention to themselves; for example:

> Sam suggested a picnic, but Sue thought the weather would be fine.
> Bill fell in love with Peg even though she was beautiful.

Assuming these sentences to be intended as written, one cannot be sure whether the writer does not know the meanings of "but" and "even though," or is confused about ordinary connections between picnics and weather, love and beauty, or is suggesting that Sue and Bill hold eccentric beliefs on these topics. In any case, although it is true that certain logical conjunctions are not learned until the late elementary school years, the principle that these conjunctions establish semantic linkages between sentences is a part of one's language competence from the preschool years.

In addition to the five just discussed, I could mention still other components of everyone's language competence. The list would read like a litany of linguistic jargon: the phonetic system and supra-segmentals, pronominalization and anaphora, the determiner system for identifying noun referents, and the various systems for affirming or negating our statements, and signaling their tense, mood, aspect, voice, and so on. Fortunately, I need not illustrate further. Instead, the important thing to remember is that five year olds *know* the principles of word order; five year olds *know* the semantic relationships, not their names but what they are; five year olds *have* lexical features ready for use in subsequent vocabulary learning; five year olds *use* sentence-combining transformations in their speech, though not nearly so many, within typical sentences, as they will later use as adults; five year olds *possess* the principle of logical conjunction.

As abstract and technical as it may sound in the linguist's terminology, language competence is nonetheless possessed by all schoolchildren from kindergarten on. They acquire it uniformly, in a way that seems independent of their intelligence (IQ), and wholly as a result of learning processess innately scheduled in every child. Moreover, these processes are beyond the reach of coaching, force-feeding, intensive corrective feedback, or other attempts at teaching. Only keeping an infant closeted from birth and deprived of all human contact could prevent the acquisition of language competence. Language competence underlies and makes possible all our uses of language. Its intricacies give eloquent testimony to the marvelous creations we humans are.

Guidelines for Teaching

To appreciate the implications for teaching that arise from the idea of language competence, we must first be certain we understand that competence is an *ability* but not a variable *skill*. Reflecting for a moment, we realize that to be considered a skill, an ability must be acquired to *differing* levels of proficiency by different people. But language competence is not. We might liken it to other invariate human abilities, for example, walking upright. Every child who is not congenitally crippled learns to walk upright, learns without teaching, and learns equally well. It does not occur to us to test people, after the age of two or thereabouts, on their ability to walk upright. That is, we have no occasion to compare their skills in doing so by observing, perhaps, that this person has not fallen down all day, whereas that one seems always in a precarious state of balance, while another keeps dropping back to all fours every few minutes. These differences simply do not exist. Nor do they exist in language competence. It is the same for all children, and offers the same springboard to school-fostered acquisition of performance skills. Now let me give the five guidelines for teaching that I think emerge from the concept of language competence.

Guideline One: Universal Readiness for Skills Learning

The first thing to remember about language competence is simply that it exists, that all children beginning school possess a sophisticated linguistic system ready for use in acquiring vocabulary and the skills of language use. To be sure, some skills development begins in the home, and may or may not have been reinforced. Vocabulary size, fluency, and motivation will differ from child to child. But no longer may we say that certain schoolchildren possess *less language* than others. No primary-grade child is deficient in grammatical structures compared with any other. Thus, the pedagogy appropriate for *all* children, not merely the intellectually and culturally favored, is a pedagogy leading students into increasingly mature uses of the linguistic system they already possess, a pedagogy showing them strategies for using the structures of their underlying competence in ever more mature patterns and combinations. Also, of course, it is a pedagogy free to move immediately into literacy education—reading and writing.

In short, teachers should recognize the large difference between saying, as we should, that all children possess the basic structures of language and need only to be taught how to utilize them in the production and comprehension of adult language, and saying, as has too often been said in the past, that some children must be formally taught those basic structures before they can "go on" to lessons in the use of more mature language. All children are ready to "go on" to language use from their first day in school. And the same thing applies to older youth right up through grade twelve. It is dead wrong, pedagogically, to encourage accomplished students to do creative writing, for example, while forcing so-called remedial students to toil away at grammar drills.

Guideline Two: The Variability of Word Learning

Second, we must preserve the distinction between language structures and words. I have just stressed that all children possess grammatical structures and the competence to acquire new vocabulary. But whereas all children know some words, the *number* they may know at any age differs widely from child to child. Furthermore, young children of every age have many more words to learn during their ensuing years in school. Most importantly, then, we must never mistakenly assume that the invariateness of language acquisition applies to the learning of words. Word learning is a process that occurs naturally but can be influenced by conscious effort and study. Presumably it is a function of both the number of words a child encounters, through talk and reading, and the spontaneity of interest and sharpness of focus with which he or she habitually attends to words newly met, and subsequently attempts to put them to active use. Presumably, too, word learning may be actively fostered. In any case, while it is incorrect to say that some young people at age thirteen or seventeen, for instance, have less language competence than others, it is by no means wrong to expect that some will have learned fewer words than others. In fact, it is often said to be more upon the extent of vocabulary development than any other variable factor that the world in general compares the accomplishments of young adults finishing school. Thus the fostering of word learning is most definitely, as good teachers have always known, a valid objective of teaching.

Guideline Three: Dialects Represent Differences, Not Deficiencies

Next it is important to recognize that the "nonstandard" dialects spoken by most children do not reflect *deficiencies* in their language competence, but are merely *differences from* the so-called standard. They are superficial in character when viewed against the underlying commonality of structure shared by all speakers of a language regardless of their dialects. Slang and actual vocabulary items aside, they are of no consequence informationally in the communication process, except that, as everyone knows, they are considered stigmatizing by middle and upper social status persons, just as nonprestige dialects always are wherever they have been known to exist.

Despite the reasonableness of the different-not-deficient view of dialects, the problem of how to treat them in schools remains unsolved. Educators have a choice, basically, between trying to change value systems and trying to teach second (standard) dialects. We know that a small percentage of persons will learn to speak a second dialect with no interference from the first, exactly as a small percentage of persons will learn to speak a second language without a trace of "foreign accent" from their first language. But we also know that most persons lack this total bilingual capability, with second dialects just as with second languages. As to the possibility of changing value systems regarding dialect differences, the problems are (a) it's never been done in the case of language values; (b) it would take generations to achieve, with no relief in the meantime to those unjustly stigmatized; and (c) it could probably be accomplished only by brainwashing or other totalitarian methods. Moreover, no matter which course educators choose, there will be damage to the self-concept of dialect speakers, resulting either from the shame and arduousness of having to learn a second dialect, or from the discrimination endured while waiting for the elite group to grow more enlightened and put away its shibboleths. So the most I can do here is underscore the point that parents and teachers must not equate possession of a nonstandard dialect either with language deficiency or with incapacity to acquire the skills of language performance. For to do either is the linguistic equivalent of racism.

Guideline Four: The Naturalness of Skills Learning

Fourth, as to the skills of language use generally and literacy in particular (the performance skills which we will shortly discuss in detail), we should bear in mind that most learning will proceed naturally and covertly in the same spontaneous manner that marked the initial acquisition of language competence. Psychologists know that the human mind is inherently disposed to extract from any piece of language it may be dealing with a knowledge of the structures and strategies involved in that piece of language. It is in this way that three year olds acquire the grammatical structures of language, and it is in this way that schoolchildren acquire, for example, most of the organizing strategies of connected discourse long before they formally study them. This is why some children learn to read without conscious effort even before starting school. In the same way, for every word a schoolchild learns to spell by rote or pictorial memorization, he or she learns one hundred through the intuition of spelling principles from reading. And in the same way, students in high school ultimately come to acquire both the vocabulary and the mental acumen necessary to recognize, talk about, and deal purposefully with mature language, entirely on their own. Given the naturalness of skills learning, therefore, it seems to me that the main responsibilities of teachers, apart from presenting certain kinds of facts and information, are the following:

> to insure, through positive response and personal affirmation, that students' desire and motivation remain high

> to provide students with opportunities to interact with (read, write, discuss) increasingly mature and purposefully chosen selections of language

> to draw to students' attention, and to help students discuss, particular aspects of language selections—idea patterns, organizational strategies, transitional words, images, tone, intention, and so on

Guideline Five: Grammar Instruction Is Not the Answer

Finally, I think we must agree that formal instruction in grammar, rhetoric, and literary concepts is *not* appropriate in the elementary and middle grades, at least not in the name of skills teaching. Some grammatical terminology is useful beginning in the junior high grades, if it is taught efficiently and without dominating the curriculum. But for the most part, the subject matters of grammar or linguistics, rhetoric, and literary criticism belong in the top two or three secondary grades only, where they can be studied systematically and at student option, as most other academic subjects are.

The main point to remember is that the learning of performance skills requires actual language use. Learning grammar also requires use of language, but on a highly abstract and technical plane. Thus it is not the *kind* of language use best suited to promoting skill development in younger children. Most adults fail to recognize this, believing that because grammar and rhetoric *pertain* to language, one not only can but must *apply* grammatical principles consciously in one's use of language, and may do so at any age. In fact, however, opportunities for conscious application of grammatical knowledge are few and far between, and elementary and most middle-school children lack the intellectual maturity necessary to do so in any case. Forcing them to try to use grammar consciously only leads to apprehension and over-cautiousness, inhibits natural skill development, and occupies time that might otherwise be devoted to language practice.

All in all, these five implications of language competence, if properly understood and pursued, can have a positive impact on teaching. But the difficulty lies in understanding. For example, I find that many persons today immediately label the suggestion that grammar drill may not be the best educational diet for all children as "soft on the basics," when in truth, one of the reasons elementary and middle-school children of average and lower aptitude don't attain targeted skill levels as quickly as we wish is that they receive *too much* rather than too little grammar and phonics drillwork. It gets in the way of real language use, real reading and writing. Presumably the best way to handle persons who believe that "Back to Basics" means an increase in old fashioned drill and memorization is to keep rubbing their noses in fact: increased phonics drills do not improve reading scores, and increased grammar drills do not improve writing ability.

Part Two: Seven Types of Language Performance Skills

In the realm of day-to-day schooling, naturally enough, it is not competence but the variable skills of language performance that occupy our concerns. In turning attention from competence to performance, I want to reiterate once more a fact which virtually all linguists and language acquisition specialists have been stressing for twenty years, but which many parents and teachers still fail to grasp: every child free of radical brain damage possesses language competence, and to possess language competence is to possess the capacity to acquire the *skills of language use*. Never should we permit ourselves to say, no matter how often we have used such phrases in the past, and no matter how poorly developed particular children's skills may seem, that such children are "language deficient," or "lack an adequate language base," or "don't have enough language." For not only is talk of this sort untrue, it triggers the chain reaction of failure—tacit belief by teachers that their teaching must fail, then acceptance by children that their attempts at learning will also fail, and finally an angry recognition by the public at large that the schools have failed. So I repeat, a child who possesses language competence possesses the capacity to learn the skills of language use.

Skills Learning and Skills Teaching

Unlike competence, however, the most obvious thing about skills development is that it does vary from child to child, both in degree of progress and schedule of onset. Moreover, we really don't know what skills are, what they "look like," as structures within the mind. For despite the advances of modern educational psychology, scholars have been unable to formulate theoretical models of the different language skills. This is a fancy way of saying that we really can't explain why some children acquire large active vocabularies, for example, whereas others in seemingly equivalent learning environments do not; why some teenagers consistently write clear coherent prose, whereas others' writing seems muddy and fragmented.

Educators have traditionally assumed that differences in skills development from student to student result partly from differences in intelligence and learning capacity, partly from differences in the quality of teaching received, and partly from differences in the degree of effort and attention with which students apply themselves. Commonsensically, this view seems true enough. In almost every classroom containing thirty students of any age, there will be some who master each skill taught in an apparently spontaneous manner. For the remainder, various degrees of conscious and sustained effort are required. And strange as it seems, although its jargon attempts to conceal the fact, educational psychology cannot take us beyond such unsophisticated notions as those just named—differential learning capacity, application, effort, and perseverance.

Differences in learning capacity, whether real or illusory, have given rise to the familiar categories of "special education"—hearing impaired, visually impaired, behavior disordered, educable mentally-handicapped, perceptually impaired, specific learning disabled, severely retarded, and so on. Factors of a different sort also enter the picture, some as inhibitants of learning, some as stimulants. Most of these are beyond the teacher's direct control—conditions in the home, quality of parenting, diet and rest, freedom from neurosis and anxiety, parental educational levels, values and attitude "set" towards schooling, peer-group mores, past successes and failures in learning, viability of hopes and future aspirations, economic stability and mental health of the family unit, and so on. In consequence, there are always two or three students in every class of thirty-odd who seem unable to master the various performance skills of language and literacy. Nor are psychologists and learning theoreticians ever really sure, except in cases of severe retardation, whether their failure results mainly from factors attributable to environment, such as those just mentioned, or whether it stems from physiological brain dysfunctions.

In any case, despite the certainty of differing environmental influences, and the possibility of structural differences in learning capacity, we should always *act as if* performance skills can be acquired by all students. Anything less becomes a self-fulfilling guarantee of nonacquisition by some. With respect to environment, we must steer a course between opposing extremes. On the one hand, if we underestimate the influence of social factors and life conditions, we risk interpreting failure to learn as a failure solely of the student's will, in which case we may respond counter-productively, by threats and exhortations, and the imposition of external pressures. This is the error into which *some* "get tough" advocates within the Back to Basics movement have fallen.

On the other hand, if we over-emphasize the role of environment, to the point where lack of learning *and* lack of motivation are excused ahead of time, particularly in the case of disadvantaged students whose lot is not of their own making, then we build a box for these young people from which there is no escape. We say to them, in effect, because you are not capable of learning and because you are not even capable of trying to learn, at least not very hard or for very long, we will dole out promotions and dole out diplomas and keep you forever on the economic dole. This policy may prevent starvation, but it also guarantees that its beneficiaries will fail to acquire even the most rudimentary skills, precisely because they will have been denied the first requisite for all school learning, namely, the belief of another that such learning is possible. Lacking the belief of another, persons never acquire the sense of dignity and self-worth on which the motivation to learn depends. Saying the same thing in different terms, a crucial *spiritual* dimension will have been missing.

Much the same is true in the teaching of children with brain impairments. Practitioners of special education have developed a vocabulary of quasi-medical terms for naming different ways a child's learning capacity may be impaired. But merely to name a problem is not to solve it, nor does the special education teacher have any "wonder drugs" to administer—only patient one-to-one teaching whose method embodies no art or magic unavailable to regular classroom teachers. And lurking just beneath the surface in every special education class is the spectre of differentness and abnormality. How teachers and students deal with this problem—for example, by denial or by admission and acceptance—can determine whether special education does a child more good than harm, or vice versa.

Questions of skills teaching involve choices between a "get tough" or an "automatic promotions" or a "special education" approach with all students but most especially with slow learners and the economically underprivileged. These are not scientific or philosophical questions at all, despite the fact that they are usually so considered, but are rather questions of pragmatics—what works? One thing we do know is that all teachers must begin by believing their students *can* attain at least minimal competence in language skills. The approaches we know *won't* succeed are those of teachers who start by saying, "These students can't learn anything."

We must also remember that merely to name the various performance skills is not to describe them substantively, certainly not to the point where foolproof teaching approaches routinely follow. Educational psychologists do *not* know how to describe the mental structures operative in skilled language use, and they do *not* know more about teaching than good teachers do—in fact, they know less. Skills teaching remains a matter in which the craft and lore of the best teachers still provide the surest guidelines for practice. The specialist's contributions lie mainly in defining the breadth and boundaries of skills learning, so that a balance may be kept in teaching, and in explaining how and why the time-serving approaches of bad teachers, silent drill and rote learning, for example, *don't* work very well.

Identifying the Language Performance Skills

Rather unfortunately, lists of language skills are ordinarily confined to one or another of the language modalities—reading, writing, literature, media, or oral language. As a result, these lists often contain a great deal of overlapping content, instances of the same thing called by different names. Skills such as understanding instructions and following directions to a place, for example, are frequently listed under oral language, as if the oral mode required a kind of skill different from those brought to bear in reading or writing the same material. Similarly, skills lists in media typically include the ability to recognize when one is being manipulated by television advertisements, as if the interpretive and critical skills involved were not exactly the same as one would use in reading those advertisements, or even in composing them. When reading specialists speak about aesthetic matters such as recognition of tone or irony, they overlap literature. When literature teachers begin by stressing literal comprehension, they overlap reading. The skills of producing and comprehending discourse structures— recognizing organizational sequences, main and supporting ideas, for instance—belong equally to reading, literature, written composition, and oral language. What the reading teacher views as a phonics and decoding matter is a question of spelling and punctuation to the writing teacher. And on and on. In the following discussion, therefore, in order to avoid this overlap problem, and to emphasize the commonality of language skills regardless of modality, I have organized the skills of language performance into the following categories:

> Communicative Skills
>
> Fluencies—Lexical, Syntactic, Creative
>
> Discourse Skills
>
> Appreciational and Critical Skills
>
> Orthographic Skills—Reading and Referencing
>
> Orthographic Skills—Mastery of the Rules of Writing
>
> Self-Governance Skills

While the names of these categories may seem new, their content will be understandable to anyone who has thought at all about the teaching and learning of language skills. I hope the novelty will lead readers to a clearer and fuller view of these skills, since nothing less will suffice if we are to arrive at enlightened answers to questions about competency.

Communicative Skills

Communicative skills are the object of current study by sociolinguists, researchers who examine language in actual social settings. Sociolinguists apply various jargony labels to their particular areas of work, such as: speech acts, oracy, registers, elaborated and restricted codes, language pragmatics, and communicative competence. The term *communicative competence* suggests exactly what some sociolinguists contend, that communicative skills are really an extension of basic language competence, since they are automatically and unconsciously learned by children during the school years, but without the aid of specific instruction. Other researchers point to evidence of variability in the timing and degree of their acquisiton, however, and suggest that these skills ought to receive attention in the elementary language curriculum.

Here are some simple examples of skills children must master. First is the ability to recognize what linguists call *entailments* and *presuppositions*. If a person says "Suzy is married," everyone immediately knows by entailment that Suzy has a husband. If someone says "Turn the light on again," its having been on before is presupposed. Somewhat similar are *conversational implicatures*, unstated agreements, so to say, in which speakers are mutually implicated. For example, because in Western cultures we consider a person's chronological age as a given fact, it violates a conversational implicature to ask "Why?" when someone states his or her age. Or if one person says "I bet I can beat you arm wrestling" and another says "So what?" neither bet nor contest is on. But if the answer is "No you can't," the bet is made.

The functions of language can also be governed by *status relations*. In the mouth of a parent, for example, the question "Whose clothes are those all over the floor?" functions as a command to a child to pick up its clothes, but the child is not free to use this form of command to an adult. Another type of utterance is called a *performative*, in which speaking the words constitutes performance of the act, as in warning, promising, dedicating, challenging, ordering, marrying, christening, and so on. Certain language functions are *situation specific*. In the classroom, for instance, children must learn the language of interrupting, turn-taking, and accepting reprimands. Sometimes cultural differences between teacher and student lead to the student's use of language formulas that are not expected by the teacher, or vice versa, and trouble can ensue.

Some sociologists study *codes*. Codes are unconscious mental systems dictating whether our language on a given occasion will be careful and elaborated, or restricted and abbreviated, depending on age differences, occupational roles, social class distinctions, and degree of shared background experiences among the speakers involved at the time. Systems similar to codes, that govern speech according to the formality/informality of the given occasion, are called *registers*. A single topic may be considered throughout a business meeting, for instance, but an individual will use one register in making a formal presentation to the group, another register in the give and take of the question and discussion session, and a third register in continuing the talk over cocktails and lunch. Similarly, as many people noted at the time, the Nixon White House tapes provided dramatic evidence that talk in a code and register appropriate to the informal conversation of associates, when transcribed and printed as public writing, often seems garbled and incomprehensible. In any case, the learning of codes and registers involves knowing when to *switch* from one code or register to another, whenever the context and occasion for speaking change, as they continually do throughout every day of our lives.

Communicative skills as a whole represent a large and complex topic whose implications for the elementary classroom are just beginning to be recognized by educators. As sociolinguists become increasingly involved in schools, we may expect the development of procedures for evaluating the language of materials written for classroom use, for diagnosing and appraising both students' and teachers' language, and for teaching about language functions where warranted. It is unclear exactly what forms of classroom practice may contribute to fuller development of communicative competence and a knowledge of language functions, but role playing, improvisations, and simulation games are likely candidates. Thusfar no one has suggested that these communicative skills be included in minimal competency tests, but research over the next decade may very well show that part of what we have until now thought of as literacy deficiencies on the part of older youth in fact stem from their imperfect knowledge of language functions.

Dialects, incidentally, do not play a role in communicative skills, since each person's dialect is a feature of his or her basic language competence. Obviously, except in cases where speakers perceive their language to be on trial at a particular moment, and thus try to modify their pronunciation or syntax for the occasion, the mono-dialectal person speaks only that one dialect regardless of code or register switching, or the requirements of language functions. Bi-dialectal persons do switch from one dialect to another according to the occasion, in much the same semi-conscious way that bi-linguals recognize which language to use in a given situation.

Unlike code and register switching, however, dialect shifting must be overtly and laboriously learned, and never becomes wholly automatic, as every bi-dialectal knows who has experienced emergence of the native (first-learned) dialect when trying to use the second in moments of anger, frustration, or fear. In any case, the main point to remember is that the dialect a student happens to speak in no way indicates whether he or she has acquired the skills of communicative competence.

Fluencies—Lexical, Syntactic, Creative

A second category of performance skills grows out of the observation that persons differ in the fluency, or facility, of their language use. *Fluency* refers to smoothness, aptness, and spontaneity of expression, to the apparent ease and readiness with which the words and structures of language come forth. In speech, quickness is a crucial attribute of fluency (response time is always a factor in tests of word fluency), but it is less important in writing. Psychologists are unable to explain why fluencies should differ from person to person, but they do agree that their development can be enhanced by practice.

The first kind of fluency is *lexical fluency*, which pertains to words and depends in large measure on vocabulary size, the number of words a person knows. Needless to say, the idea of "knowing" a word can be defined in many ways, only one of which is the ability to identify its synonym on a multiple-choice vocabulary test. In the preschool years the lexical richness of the home language is assumed to be the main factor governing word learning, although television and one's peer group are also sources. Once schoolchildren learn to read, teachers observe that some students become veritable "word sponges" who not only infer meanings easily from context, but tend to remember such words once learned. Other children seem to lack this tendency, so that by the late elementary grades rather wide differences in vocabulary knowledge can be noted among children of otherwise equivalent aptitude, who have sat side by side in the same classrooms for a number of years.

Word-by-word vocabulary study becomes appropriate in the secondary grades, though it falls a distant third, behind wide reading and study in the content areas, as a source of word learning. Despite the fact that separate vocabulary study is unpopular with many educational theorists, presumably because it seems old fashioned and mechanical, we have no experimental evidence, one way or the other, as to its effectiveness. Certainly, like anything else, it is wrong if practiced to excess or made a drudgery. We do know, from common knowledge, that adults possessing many words—whether crossword puzzle buffs, poets, or ordinary people whose vocabularies happen to be large—are generally at home with dictionaries and reference books, whereas their opposite numbers frequently are not. In any case, in addition to regular spelling lessons, which serve to teach vocabulary every bit as much as spelling, teachers in the middle school and secondary grades are well advised to teach their students roots, prefixes, etymologies, compounds, derivational groupings, new coinages, borrowings from other languages, and the like, in a systematic way, and to establish expectations for students regarding dictionary use and mastery tests in connection with unfamiliar words encountered while reading.

A second kind of fluency is *syntactic fluency*, which is more notable in writing than in speech simply because written sentences on average, from the secondary grades through adulthood, are more elaborated structurally than are spoken ones. Syntactic fluency pertains to the ease and skill with which one uses sentence-combining transformations, either automatically or consciously, to include within each full sentence all the ideas one wishes to include, cast in forms that are stylistically appropriate and grammatically correct. Syntactic fluency in writing depends upon short-term memory and the willingness to reflect upon and craft one's utterances. It can be enhanced by specific practice requiring the combination of numbers of short simple sentences into single more elaborated ones. More and more teachers now see the wisdom of asking junior and senior high school students to devote five or ten minutes daily to sentence-combining practice in one form or another to further develop their syntactic fluency. It is likely too that syntactic fluency plays a role in reading as well as in writing, since the sentences of any text must somehow be reconstructed in the reader's mind in the act of comprehension, much as they are by the writer in the act of composing.

The third kind of fluency is *creative fluency*, or more simply, *creativity*. Creative fluency manifests itself in the inventing and casting of ideas in ways that match dissimilars, that are novel and unexpected, spontaneous and apt, memorable and effective. Metaphor-making and the solving of problems in unusual ways are further indicators of creativity. Most psychologists agree that creativity cannot be taught, though it may perhaps be enhanced. Nobody quite understands why some minds seem naturally more creative than others. Coming to value the novel over the prosaic may stimulate some persons to "wait longer" in speaking and writing, until a truly arresting idea has had time to develop. Other persons may need to be rewarded for giving voice to their first thoughts, since these are sometimes more creative than ones pondered too long. To heighten creative fluency, many elementary teachers have students play word association games, write metaphors and similes about familiar concepts, invent strange new uses for ordinary objects, and strive to make bizarre comparisons among dissimilars. To date, however, a person's creative fluency has been considered sufficiently invariable to warrant its exclusion from standardized achievement tests, and presumably it will be omitted from competency tests also.

Discourse Skills

When we speak or write, we do not direct individual words or sentences to one another, we discourse. A *discourse* is any piece of language, written or spoken, ranging in length from one sentence to thousands of sentences, defined by three distinctive attributes: a recognizable authorial purpose, a namable subject treated in a form that is structurally whole, and an intentional quality identifying it as meant for a definite audience or recipient. Discourse structure has been studied since the time of Aristotle, who termed authorial purpose *ethos*, topical content *logos*, and audience bias *pathos*. In *discoursing*, as the process of producing or comprehending language has come to be called, persons use not only their basic language competence, but also their unconscious knowledge of language patterns larger than the sentence, along with everything else they know, or *cognize*, that is relevant to the occasion. This is why some scholars today consider discourse study a part of cognitive psychology.

Many schemes exist for classifying types of discourse. One of these divides discourse into three broad categories by purpose: transactional (more familiarly called expository), expressive, and literary. *Transactional* discourses are either informational or conative (persuasive or regulatory). Informational discourses aim to record, report, characterize, define, analyse, classify, compare, distinguish, reason logically to conclusions, explain, exemplify, analogize, generalize, or theorize. Conative discourses seek to instruct, recommend, demand, legislate, regulate, judge, advocate, argue, or persuade. Opposite to the transactional are *literary* discourses, whose subject matter is imaginative and fictive, whose mode is narrative or dramatic or lyric, and whose aesthetic features may be poetic. Literary discourses, as readers of literature know full well, often are conative in underlying purpose. Between the transactional and the literary are *expressive* discourses, which tend to be unstable as to purpose and form, unstructured, and to reflect the continuously variable state of human intention. Much of our daily talk consists of expressive discourses.

To acquire discourse skills is to acquire the complex mental structures enabling us, as speakers and writers, to connect sentences into larger linguistic wholes, sometimes loosely called "blocs" or "chunks." Psycholinguists refer to discourse skills as *cognitive macro-structures* by means of which we relate the temporal flow of sentences into integrated hierarchies of thought. Simply put, what happens with words at the sentence level also happens with sentences at the discourse level: just as the syntactic structures of language allow us to understand a sequence of words that mean different things if taken separately as *one* thing when combined in a sentence, so do our discourse skills enable us to understand a sequence of sentences that would mean separate things if viewed apart from one another as meaning *one* thing when connected in a single piece of discourse. Discourse skills thus constitute what might be termed a "grammar of thought."

As with communicative competence, the study of discourse skills, or discourse processing, is relatively new and quite active. Never at a loss for newfangled jargon, psycholinguists have coined many names for their various lines of inquiry: cohesion and cohesive ties, textlinguistics, proposition analysis, rheme and theme relationships, discourse blocs, story grammars, inference networks, schemata, conceptual dependencies, and so on. All of these represent attempts to describe human understanding in terms of general structures of thought. Obviously we cannot examine these different approaches here, since they are complicated and comprehensive.

Throughout the twelve years of school and even beyond, young people busily but for the most part unknowingly acquire both the cognitive "life knowledge" and the mental, logical, and organizational competencies that make discourse skills possible. Without these, people would be little more than random sentence generators, utterly unable to produce (speak or write), comprehend (hear or read), or even think about connected meaning. While the acquisition of discourse skills is mostly unconscious, the rate and extent of learning can differ from student to student at any given time. Certain classroom activities can promote the development of discourse skills, activities in which teachers illustrate and analyse the structure of written passages, call students' attention to relevant features, précis and paraphrase idea content, provide vocabulary necessary for talking about discourse structure, and assign exercises calling for the speaking and writing of discourses of many types addressed to many different hypothetical audiences.

When composition teachers display familiar forms of paragraph and essay structure (classification, definition, process, cause and effect, and so on), and when they teach transitional words and phrases, they are teaching discourse skills. When reading teachers illustrate how the meaning of a recurring concept expands as a text progresses, or when they chart idea sequences and ask for statements of main idea, they are teaching discourse skills. When students read or write almost anything at all, or talk and discuss, or think in any way, they are exercising and developing their discourse skills. No less stupendous a feat than the preschool acquisition of language competence, the development of discourse skills, including as it must the ongoing acquisition of general knowledge and vocabulary, is by far the largest single piece of learning children accomplish during their school years, bar none. Beyond the questions of orthography discussed below, most of the things that language achievement tests measure are aspects of discourse skill. We may *call* them tests of reading or writing, but in actuality they measure discourse skills.

Appreciational and Critical Skills

Two subgroupings of discourse skills that reading and English teachers consider especially important are appreciational skills and critical skills. *Appreciational* skills cover logical inference and the ability to grasp anything and everything that the maker of a discourse (a speaker or a writer) does not explicitly state but means to convey through tone, mood, irony, wit, innuendo, flattery, sarcasm, anger, gesture, and body language. Of central importance are metaphor and other kinds of imagery, whose meanings, as literary scholars have pointed out, "fill in the gaps" between the boundaries of what it is possible to say in literal language. Appreciational skills also include perception of essentially aesthetic (artistic) features of discourses—rhythms in sound, syntax, and sense that guide and enrich understanding, and give pleasure through the sensory impressions they create. Turns of phrase, balances, antitheses, emphasis of various sorts, stylistic patternings, particular word choices —all these contribute to the appreciation of artistry in verbal discourse, both spoken and written.

Critical skills, in turn, inform one's judgmental and evaluative responses to discourses. A person may judge many aspects of a particular passage: its logic may be weak or faulty; its claim to fact may be untrue; authorities cited may be questionable; it may overgeneralize in its conclusion or marshall insufficient evidence; it may employ persuasive or propagandist devices one finds transparent; or it may simply collapse under scrutiny. Or, it may hold or advocate points of view repugnant to the respondent, such as ideas that violate one's beliefs, ethical standards, or sense of priorities or values. Or, finally, the aesthetic features of the discourse may be flawed in numerous ways, so that the intended artistry does not work; it may cause us to wince instead of enjoy, or worse yet, to die of boredom. On the other hand, a particular discourse may reveal such fullness of idea and such pleasing form, such strength of argument and flashing insight, that our senses are quickened and our critical responses steered toward judgments of brilliance, beauty, timelessness, truth. In any case, all the judgmental and evaluative responses we give to discourses, both heard and read, are made possible by the application of our critical skills.

As to matters of testing, it is important to recognize that critical and appreciational responses to pieces of discourse *are themselves discourses*—passages of language we think or say or write in response to other passages said or written to us. Therefore, the skills at work in criticism and appreciation, apart from whatever knowledge we possess about the thing we are critiquing or appreciating, are nothing more or less than the discourse skills just discussed. When test specialists in reading and/or literature, as they ordinarily do, place critical and appreciational skills in a hierarchy superior to and apparently different from discourse skills, they obscure this fundamental fact. Much more harmful is to regard appreciational skills as pertaining to "literature" but not to "reading." Despite instances of overlap, we know that expository and literary discourses generally differ from one another in form and subject matter. Both, however, convey their makers' intentions through devices going beyond literal statement, and both are subject to appreciational responses and critical appraisal.

The upshot of all this is that it is very bad testing (and teaching) practice to speak of reading as if it did not extend to literature, or of literature as if it did not include reading. Similarly, it would be a great mistake, in any kind of a competency test, to exclude the measurement of critical and appreciational skills, in response to discourses that are nonliterary as well as literary, on grounds that these skills are somehow of less practical value than are the skills of so-called "literal comprehension." If anything, the reverse is true. In short, when we critique and appreciate any discourse, we too are engaging in the act of discoursing, and the skills we bring to bear are discourse skills, which deserve to be so recognized and so tested. We should remember most especially that one's critical and appreciational responses to any piece of discourse lead to meanings that are at least as important as the meanings one derives from its literal comprehension, and that are therefore a crucial part of one's overall interpretation and understanding of the piece.

Orthographic Skills—Reading and Referencing

Much of schooling is devoted to teaching children to process language by eye rather than by ear. From the perspective of the teacher of beginning reading, this is first a matter of establishing certain *visual orientations*: left to right, top to bottom, between-word versus between-letter spacings, recognition of the printed and cursive alphabets, capital versus lower-case letters, and punctuation. Second, there is the teaching of *letter-sound correspondence* and *word identification*. Third and finally is the sometimes brief, sometimes agonizingly protracted period during which the child is urged, coached, and exhorted to leave word identification behind and to commence *automatic reading*, which is the skill of comprehending orthographic text in the same natural, easy, and effortless manner as one comprehends the flow of oral language.

With the exception of the referencing skills I shall mention in a moment, the three orthographic concerns just outlined exhaust the teaching of reading *per se*. Despite this fact, reading specialists ordinarily include in their lists of "reading skills" aspects of language processing that are the same for speech as for print—for example, syntactic and semantic comprehension, interpretation of discourse structure, and the making of critical and appreciational responses. Psycholinguists offer varying hypotheses as to how language is recognized and processed by the mind, but they agree that whatever happens "behind the eye and beyond the ear" is the same regardless of whether the physical medium of the received language is sound or writing, that is, whether the sending signal is acoustic or visual.

In any case, the real accomplishment in learning to read is the quantum leap from word identification to automatic reading. A few precocious children make the transition entirely on their own prior to schooling. Some do so in a period of weeks in response to coaching by teachers, while others require two years and sometimes more to go from words to reading. Older nonreaders, unless brain damaged, are persons who have been unable to master this crucial skill. Absolutely essential though it is, automatic reading is the one reading skill *that no one knows how to teach*! Beginning readers are wholly on their own in figuring out how to stop reading words, and to begin comprehending text. Since its beginnings, research on methods of teaching reading has shown that no method works for all children and every method works for some. The reason for these peculiar findings is that none of the existing methods comprehends this mysterious "shift of awareness" from individual words to textual meanings, a shift that hallmarks automatic reading.

For over a century psychologists have been conducting tachistoscopic studies of reading. Although researchers do not know what *does* happen in the reading process, they have a good idea of what does *not*. Automatic readers do not "stop" to identify letters or words. They do not decode print into speech. In a covert process that cannot be measured by any physical process thusfar devised, the mind "takes" from the optical percept (the image in the eye) a meaning that is "matched" with internally generated concepts that dictate what the reader recognizes. Moreover, recent studies of miscues (errors) in proficient oral reading confirm that reading aloud is governed by prior comprehension of sentence meaning rather than a word-by-word, letter-sound-to-phonetics conversion of printed text to oral speech.

As a result, current psycholinguistic teaching advice runs counter to conventional classroom practice. Teachers need *not*, for example, invoke phonics rules and require single-word identification when a reader gets stalled. They need *not* penalize eye and voice regressions. They need *not* downgrade guessing or call attention to oral reading mistakes. In general, unless the young reader has been conditioned by well-intentioned but wrongly directed instruction to concentrate on decoding, whatever he or she is doing, quite unconsciously of course, represents an attempt by the mind to escape from the level of conscious attention to orthography, where comprehension is frustrated, and to ascend to the plateau of automatic reading, where the processing and fullscale comprehension of text occurs as naturally and spontaneously as does the comprehension of accoustically transmitted language— whether speech, or writing read aloud.

In addition to reading *per se*, students must master several kinds of *referencing skills*, activities made possible by the fact that orthographic text remains static before the eye. Whenever persons read, the manner of their reading is governed by their purpose and the nature of the text. Thus they may speed up, slow down, reread, focus attention selectively, or stop to study, ponder, paraphrase, or respond to what they are reading by reference to what they already know and believe about the topic. These referencing behaviors are often called *study skills*. Another form of referencing involves *locational skills*, which include knowledge about indexes, tables of contents, alphabetical listing, dictionaries and the many other kinds of reference books, and library organization.

Still another kind of referencing pertains to knowledge of *specialized formats*. On one hand there are materials wherein the language content may be coded figurally or numerically rather than exclusively in line-by-line print. Examples are maps, tables, charts, graphs, plans, blueprints, diagrams, exploded drawings, and so forth. On the other hand are passages of language whose print content is arrayed nonlinearly in visually peculiar formats, as in information forms of all kinds, personal and business letters, mail-order catalogues, TV guides, recipes, packaging labels, want ads, checkbook ledgers, invoices, bills and charge account statements, grade report forms from schools, contracts, bank statements, and on and on.

Study and locational skills have conventionally been taught in schools, along with "regular" reading. But specialized formats have not, because competent readers have always been able to interpret these special formats on their own. Recently, however, perhaps in an attempt to make their test items more real-worldly in appearance, and thus to seem of greater practical importance, commercial test-makers have included increasing numbers of special-format items in their test batteries. Predictably, given the added pressures imposed by examination conditions, and the nature of the exam as a simulation not a reality, many young people have been unable to answer questions based on special-format texts, with the result that teachers are being pressured to teach these formats in schools. We may hope that teachers will resist these pressures, however, since what needs to be taught is not formats but fluent reading and wider vocabulary. Fluent readers, whose skill enables them readily to comprehend the language contained in special-format texts, will almost immediately grasp the plan of the special format. *Teaching* such plans would seem, in most cases, to occupy time that might better be used in guided reading practice. This is merely an assumption, of course, and should be tested.

On the whole, despite huge amounts of money spent annually on reading instruction, one of the most alarming conditions in education today is the number of functional illiterates in our high schools. Apart from cases of brain damage or dysfunction (dyslexia), these are students who, after eight years in school, still have not acquired the skill of automatic reading. Nearly all these students avoid reading whenever possible, associating it with frustration, embarrassment, and increasing irrelevance to their lives. Most have never experienced the supreme pleasure of engrossment, of entering so completely into the world of a book, whether fiction, biography, history, or science, that the reality of its language becomes for a time one's only reality, and its meaning the sole source of one's imaginings, to the exclusion of any awareness whatever of the reading act as a conscious mental process.

Reading specialists freely admit our lack of knowledge as to why these older youth seem unable to master automatic reading, but they are less willing to go the next step and at least consider the possibility that conventional methods of reading instruction actually *work against* such mastery. After all, high school nonreaders have spent eight years in the elementary grades performing various kinds of drill and study whose net effect has been to persuade them that the act of reading consists of the serial identification of words, when in fact it consists of the automatic comprehension of text.

Analogies are never perfect and this one has been used before, but learning to read in many ways resembles learning to ride a bicycle. You cannot *tell* someone how to balance a two-wheeler. You cannot *explain* how to keep it upright, or break the process down into steps. Most youngsters learn spontaneously, enough so that those who don't—who keep being wheeled around and held up, forced to try when they're tired of trying, launched down the sidewalk only to fall off and bruise their knees and their dignity in front of everyone—soon develop blocks and hangups they remember all their lives, and that further frustrate their learning.

But worst of all, in learning to bike ride, are the training wheels. With training wheels, you can't start up right, and you can't lean into turns. Even going straight, they touch ground every now and then and throw your balance off. You can never forget you're using them. A few youngsters do learn to ride with the training wheels still on, but everybody knows they're really riding tricycles, and so do they. And the longer they stay with training wheels, the more frightened they are to try without them, for fear of falling and being ridiculed.

The "training wheels" of reading instruction are the following: phonics drills and games, flash cards, texts accompanied by informationally synonymous pictures, the distracting rhymes in so-called "linguistic" texts (Dan gave Nan a tan fan), mini-text "rate builders" in reading kits, and all kinds of mechanical devices that present the reading act as other than the visual scanning of uninterrupted page-length print. The difference is that training wheels never stay on bicycles very long, whereas in reading instruction they are all that our older nonreaders have ever known, apart from guessing at answers to comprehension questions and having regularly to give oral demonstrations of their semi-literacy.

It is fair to say, I think, that most of the functional illiterates in our secondary schools do not need competency testing or any more time with training wheels. What they *do* need is an hour or more a day alone with an adult, a skillful tutor who can get the right reading material into their hands, deactivate their avoidance and defense mechanisms, praise and encourage every positive attemp they make no matter how badly it miscarries, then "walk alongside them" as they read, nudging them away from attacking words and towards daring to inhale whole sentences, tolerating regressions and pauses signifying silent rereading, knowing when to provide a pronunciation or meaning, when to ask for rereading of a miscue and (more often) when not to, when to choral read, when to have the reader switch from oral to silent or back to oral, when to stop and when to start again, always remembering to affirm, affirm, affirm. Again, competency testing is unnecessary, because teachers know who their nonreaders are. What *is* needed is an improved, perhaps even a radically different, approach to teaching. "Quantity practice" by itself is certainly not the answer, and that is not what I am suggesting. What we do need is less fussing over transitory phonics problems, less reliance on commercial gimmicks and devices, and greater emphasis on real books and one-to-one student-tutor interaction. Such an approach would be "radical" in the true sense of the term, a sense that would take us back to the root form in which teaching and learning occur.

Orthographic Skills—Mastery of the Rules of Writing

On the surface, at least, the first problem a child must deal with in learning to write his or her language is figuring out how to spell its words. A few children who take up writing before learning to read invent surprisingly regular though wholly unorthodox spelling systems on their own. Most students, of course, first learn to spell as a by-product of their initial reading instruction. The same is true for punctuation and capitalization. Much writing throughout the younger years continues to be plagued by orthographic faults— both accidental mistakes and regular deviations from convention— until the end of high school. Formal instruction and drillwork are typically begun in the elementary grades and continued throughout the secondary years. Interestingly enough, however, we have no evidence whatever that the correctness level of twelfth graders' writing is one bit higher than it would have been had drillwork been deferred until the eleventh grade, then assigned on a prescription basis as needed. In fact, the latter approach has never been tried.

A second difficulty in learning to write is purely physical, stemming from the fact that in composing, one's flow of thought far exceeds the speed at which one's hand can inscribe the words on paper. The problem is especially acute with younger children whose motor skills are still developing, and accounts for the fact that their oral sentences are longer, on average, than their written ones throughout the elementary grades, after which their written sentences grow longer. Two important performance skills that must be mastered, therefore, are two-channel thinking and decentering. In *two-channel thinking*, a person learns to inscribe what is being written at the moment while simultaneously storing in memory what has arisen in verbal consciousness but is yet to be written down. Some writers develop a variant of this skill, learning to hold their thought in abeyance and control its rate of flow without stemming it. But nothing is more shattering than to hear in one's mind a sudden torrent of wonderful words, only to be paralysed by the fear that they will be forgotten before they can be written, and thus to lose them. The skill of *decentering* is also vital, in that it allows the writer to "stand apart" from whatever has been written, whether a sentence or two or a complete discourse, and to regard it objectively as something totally under one's control, an artifact to be crafted and shaped to conformity with both the dictates of the writer's thought and the needs of the reading audience. Without the skills of two-channel thinking and decentering, it is doubtful that persons could write at all.

The third problem presented by writing really has nothing to do with orthography, though it turns on an essential difference between the written and the spoken language. Speech is naturally learned and (most of the time) performed without conscious effort. Writing, however, utilizes a somewhat different and more extensive vocabulary, is bereft of intonation and the paralinguistic channels afforded language users who are in visual and vocal contact, is generally more extended in length, is likely though not necessarily more abstract in level of discourse (exposition, focused argumentation, and so on), is cluttered with more rhetorical "signposts" and devices of transition and cohesion, and consists of deeply embedded semantic structures in which relations of parts to wholes must be signaled by explicit verbal devices. All of these factors help explain why writing is cognitively more demanding than talking. Moreover, despite recent attempts by educators to eliminate the need for pretense in school writing, it continues to be true that successful student writers are those who learn to make their essays seem self-initiated rather than teacher-imposed, and to write them as if intended for an unknown public audience when in reality the audience is just the classroom teacher, or at best, the teacher and a few classmates.

At this point, lest readers wonder why I am not discussing types of writing—for example, expository (transactional), expressive, or "creative" (literary)—or various organizational sequences, paragraph structures, and what not, I should reiterate that all of these things are functions of the discourse skills already described. Matters such as mode of discourse, organization, and relation of content and form are governed by one's discourse skills, whether the language modality at a particular moment happens to be speech or writing. Obviously, the problems in *producing* a discourse, especially in writing, seem cognitively more difficult than those involved in "merely" *comprehending* one that someone else has produced, since writers must first discover (invent and/or collect) their ideas, then decide how to order them and cast them into sentences. Paradoxically, perhaps, preliminary writing can be as effective a means to this end as is reading or thinking about the topic, or discussing it with others. In fact, many writers claim they don't learn what they want to write on a given topic until they write about it. In any event, the discourse skills discussed earlier in this chapter are brought to bear as fully in writing as in any other mode of language use.

This is not to say there are no special performance skills writers must learn. Far from it. The following list summarizes seven general skills that beginning writers must master: *One*, knowing how to introduce a topic, hence begin an essay, as if the ideas expressed were put forward *on the writer's own initiative* rather than in response to an externally-imposed topic question. *Two*, knowing how to employ the many transitional/referential devices (also called cohesion ties) required in writing, whose function is to tag and render verbally explicit the ideational structure of any piece of extended discourse. *Three*, knowing how to draw to a close a piece of writing by means of the many appropriate strategies the written language uses to signal endings and conclusions. *Four*, knowing which words of the spoken language (especially coterie slang, conversational and juvenile locutions, and expressive intrusions of other sorts) are barred from the registers of formal writing, unless used intentionally for effect. *Five*, knowing how to achieve a particular writing style or styles, largely through tonal concordances in vocabulary choice, and rhythmic repetitions of syntactic structures and idea patterns; and knowing when to shift styles. *Six*, knowing how to recognize and meet the informational needs of a general and undifferentiated reading audience, as distinct from those of a known correspondent or one or more auditors present in a speech situation. *Seven*, knowing how to conform to the mechanical conventions (rules) of standard orthography (spelling, punctuation, capitalization, syntactic form, manuscript form, and so forth).

Altogether, it is clear that the "rules of writing" are numerous and wide-ranging. But this is no reason to conclude that they need necessarily be laboriously identified and cataloged, taught individually, or drilled singly, anymore than is the case with the grammatical forms of sentences. Nor can writing ability be validly tested on a one-skill-at-a-time basis, or by reference to a single sample of a writer's work—a matter more fully discussed in the chapter on writing later in this book.

Self-Governance Skills

Quite obviously, the performance skills of language are not acquired in a psychological vacuum. Regardless of whether classroom activities involve formal study (for example, understanding the concept of passive voice), conscious analysis (identifying the plot line of a short story), or less constrained forms of language use (free reading or participation in a small group discussion), they all require focused attention, sustained involvment, and an overall motivational state in which the student either positively desires to pursue the activity through to completion, or, if not positively desirous, is at least willing to do so more or less unstintingly.

Putting it simply, most learning activities in school require effort and staying power. And many of them are work—sometimes exhilarating, sometimes drudgery; sometimes boring, sometimes fun. For a variety of reasons, some justified some not, many students are unwilling, or perhaps unable, to invest themselves in the work of learning, or to persevere to any appreciable extent. In writing, for example, two of the most important keys to success are, first, the willingness to spend sufficient time in the discovery of content (called prewriting), and in planning and rough-drafting its composition, before producing the final version; and second, the habit of rehearsing elements of one's sentences repeatedly in mind during and after their inscription, and of stopping frequently to reread and contemplate and reformulate what one has written. Both of these behaviors require self-control and work.

Also important in language learning is the willingness to accept a teacher's criticism and corrective feedback without letting them lower one's self concept, generate animosity, or kill motivation—

no small feat, as everyone who has spent even one day in school well remembers! Similarly, successful learners are persons willing to take risks and to try out new modes of expression, to initiate projects on their own and tackle seemingly insurmountable tasks, and to revise or begin again without losing heart when their first efforts go astray or fall short of the mark.

At the beginning of this discussion, I stressed the point that educators must always *act as if* the skills of language performance can be acquired by all children, regardless of the many psychological and sociological reasons why, in particular cases, such acquisition may be difficult to bring about. Now I would say the same thing about self-governance skills. Classroom teachers may be aware of a hundred legitimate reasons why a certain child could be excused from the requirements of trying, paying attention, conforming to norms of group behavior, accepting criticism, and so on. But to remove these requirements, or to fail to levy them, to lower to zero one's expectations of the child in the realm of self-governance, is to insure that the child will make no attempt whatever to meet them, on occasions either for learning or for test-taking. As every teacher knows, the trickiest part of teaching is the setting of appropriate expectations for each student being taught—learning expectations to be sure, but along with those, appropriate expectations of self-governance. Society can and must provide, the family can and must nurture, the teacher and the curriculum can and must motivate, but only the child can decide to attend, to focus, to try, and to keep on trying.

Conclusion

I began this chapter by describing language competence, the basic knowledge of linguistic structure that all children acquire en route from crib to schoolroom. Language competence is knowledge learned through a completely natural process of which no child is consciously aware, a process beyond the influence of formal instruction in grammatical principles or special drillwork of any kind. Preschool children acquire language because their minds are innately structured to do so. All that is required is that the infant be reared in a human environment wherein language is spoken. This is true for all children. If it were possible to administer a minimal competence language test to five year olds (which is about what language acquisition research boils down to), *all* children except the grossly brain-damaged would pass with flying colors.

Turning from competence to performance, I then delineated seven types of performance skills acquired during the school years: communicative skills, fluencies, discourse skills, critical and appreciational skills, orthographic skills utilized in reading and writing, and the psychological skills of self-governance necessary to support the learning process. Here too, most of the relevant learning proceeds in the same natural manner that characterizes the initial acquisition of competence. True, vocabulary and conceptual structures are learned by reading and other experiences in the different fields of knowledge, some vocabulary can be consciously learned word by word, certain orthographic skills can be honed through drill, features of discourse can be pointed to and labeled, analytic tasks can be performed, some rules of writing can be overtly studied, and young people can, through self-discipline, increase the amount of effort they invest in their studies. But the general rule is that performance skills are learned through use of language, *not* as a result of formal instruction, drillwork, or direct conceptual teaching. Indeed, theoretical formulations learned in a vacuum, whether grammatical, rhetorical, or literary, are as irrelevant to skills development as is memorizing the telephone book.

In short, one cannot *tell* a child how to shift from word identification to real reading. One cannot *tell* a child how to compose a written discourse on a certain topic, since once a pattern or content is given, the child is no longer composing but merely grafting content onto a set structure or vice versa. One cannot *tell* a child what critical responses to make, or how to appreciate. Young people do not learn automatic reading by applying phonics principles faster. Young people do not learn to write cumulative sentences by identifying coordinate participles and nominative absolutes. They do not learn formal vocabulary registers by memorizing long lists of words, and they do not learn to make rational and incisive arguments by defining major and minor premises. Instead, young people learn language skills by using language naturally. They learn to read by reading, to write by writing, and to argue by arguing.

Self-selected reading, writing, and discussing represent one kind of language use. Other learning activities, such as sentence-combining exercises, looking up word meanings, writing essays on assigned topics, reading teacher-suggested material the typical child might never choose on his or her own, and answering a teacher's instructional questions, while ususally not self-sponsored, constitute another equally natural kind of language use, whose only contrivance lies in their having been selected by the teacher on grounds that they bring into use the *particular forms* of language whose processing triggers the acquisition and development of specific performance skills.

Again and again we must stress a central truth: the learning of performance skills occurs in an integrated, wholistic, and largely nonconscious way, as a result of the child's organic predisposition towards such learning. Not only is there little point (except as an academic exercise) in attempting to draw up an exhaustive and explicit list of these performance skills, but to try to teach them singly would be to frustrate learning completely. As a matter of fact, skills learning would occur to a considerable extent even if schools did not exist, so long as children were not entirely cut off from language interaction with the adult linguistic cultures towards which they are heading. In other words, there is no specific subject matter that teaches language skills, there can only be a rich variety of occasions for actual language use.

As already suggested, however, planned curriculum-wide programs of in-school language use do serve important functions. One is to insure that students experience the right *forms* of language use, organized in the right *sequences*, and followed up by the right kinds of purposeful and corrective *feedback*. Their second function is to introduce as the overt *objects* of classroom study certain bodies of organized knowledge (educators call it "content"), such that the purpose of the students' language use, at least in part, will seem to be that of transacting with (learning, analyzing, discussing, manipulating, applying, and so on) the particular body of knowledge, rather than empty practice on skills. In other words, science, mathematics, social studies, literature, and the other content fields are important to the language specialist mainly because of the opportunities they present for students to exercise their language performance skills without becoming aware that that is what they are doing. The first function is important because it guarantees that the students' language performance will bring into play various vocabulary registers, language functions, and types of discourse, the exercise of the different fluencies, opportunities to make critical and appreciational judgments, and regular use of the orthographic modalities (reading and writing). The second function serves to keep the language use natural; it prevents students from self-consciously focusing upon their language *as* language, such that their use of it, and therefore their skills development, would be inhibited.

What then of competency testing in the various language modalities? Here I think the main question is not whether competency tests are good or bad, since on their face they are no different from the familiar achievement tests that most schools administer yearly in one form or another. Nor can we dispute the claim, at least not at the high school level, that real skills deficiencies exist. We know full well that significant numbers of students, having been identified as "deficient" or "below grade level" in this or that language skill at differing points in their grade schooling, and having been shunted into "remedial" or "special" curriculums to receive direct "skills" instruction, nevertheless approach twelfth grade graduation still remedial, still far below grade level. These are the truly "deficient," who are definitely below the level of minimal competence one might reasonably expect of young people who have attended twelve years of school. So the key question really is, it seems to me, what's wrong with our minimal competency *teaching*? Why aren't our remedial language skills programs working?

Putting the same thing slightly differently, there is nothing wrong with our *definitions* of language competence and the skills of language performance, and nothing (at least I think nothing fundamental) wrong with our *tests* of these skills. But there is something terribly wrong with our methods of *teaching* them in cases where students have been identified as remedial or deficient. Our skills teaching works fine with mainstreamers, but once a boy or girl is slated for placement in any of the thousand different remedial programs found in our schools today, however euphemistically it may be named, and whatever its grade level, something seems to go wrong. But what?

The answer has three parts, any or all of which may apply in the case of a particular student. First, as I have already pointed out, we prescribe the wrong kind of pedagogy: almost always some form of "direct" skills teaching, a frontal assault in which the principal subject matter is the rules and terminology describing the skills themselves. Students become more and more isolated from one another, working in booths and kits and programmed workbooks and individualized learning packets. Occasions for real language use diminish. Where they do occur they seem increasingly like empty exercises or tests. The result is an increase in self-consciousness—which in its most profound sense is the deadly enemy of every kind of human development—and a decrease in the "naturalness" of language use, both of which retard rather than stimulate skills acquisition. In short, we switch from a pedagogy in which learning occurs because we *permit* it to occur, to one in which we try to *coerce* learning, to *force* it to occur, only to find, paradoxically, that we have frustrated it.

Second, in switching students from mainstream to remedial teaching, we telegraph to these young people the erroneous belief that something is wrong with them, or at least wrong with their condition. In speaking about these students we begin to use terms such as "problem," "handicap," "weakness," "deficiency," "failure," and that most misleading and pernicious phrase in all of American elementary education, "below grade level." Again and again, in the case of particular language skills, we view later-than-average time of onset, and slower-than-average rate of development, as quasi-medical pathologies needing "diagnosis" and some kind of "cure," when in fact they are merely the normal outworkings of developmental schedules that vary naturally from person to person, in exactly the same way that things such as onset of puberty, or rate of growth in height, vary widely from one individual to another. Being "below grade level" in reading, for example, merely means being below the arithmetic average of one's chronological age-mates. Obviously, in any large group, roughly half of all children will be below average at any given time, and half above average. But unless they are otherwise psychically crippled (in which case teaching *per se*, whether remedial or regular, is no help at all), *all* are progressing at a pace appropriate to each. To attempt direct skills teaching to students whose natural learning schedules happen to be slower and later than those of the majority of their peers, and to label their condition as pathological, however good our intentions and rational our approach, is in fact to confront these children with twin roadblocks to their learning. Thus we see that absurdity is not confined to literature and the stage: it is alive and well in our remedial language curriculums.

Third is the situation arising from what we may call "ghetto prejudice." Students victimized by ghetto prejudice live not only in our inner cities but on Indian reservations and in many remote and rural places. They may be black or Hispanic or recent immigrants whose first languge is not English, or they may be none of these. But almost certainly they suffer from economic poverty and the environmental savaging that throughout time has been poverty's bestial handmaid. In schools and classrooms where students are poor and ghetto prejudice prevails, there *is* no mainstream teaching. Children are not switched into remedial programs, they start out in them. Despite occasional exceptions and well-meant protestations to the contrary, teachers look upon ghetto students as deficient from the beginning. The ordinary presumption of natural skills learning is simply never made. Students in wholesale lots are assumed not only to be late and slow in skills development, but to possess little or no potentiality for such development, to be essentially hopeless cases. As a result, direct remedial teaching in an atmosphere of futility is the only kind of teaching that occurs. The assumed deficits soon become quite real, cumulate from year to year, and harden into truth.

But responsibility for our failure at skills teaching is by no means limited to teachers and school personnel alone. For it also lies with the handful of large corporations which, within the past ten to fifteen years, have acquired control of the educational publishing business as a sales outlet for their technological hardware. Their procedure has been to fragment the skills of language into smaller and smaller sub-divisions, knowing that each new organization gives them the opportunity to market yet another "learning system," with its computers, machines, kits, manuals, packets, drillbooks, diagnostic checklists, and continuous mastery progress charts. Systematic approaches like these may be fine for imparting information and teaching content, but language skills *lack* an essential content, do *not* consist of information, and resist piecemeal teaching.

Responsibility also lies with the many college and university educationists who have permitted concepts of programmed learning, behavioral objectives, and performance criteria—good ideas for teaching content—to apply to the organization of remedial language skills programs. In so doing, they have given publishers a cloak of theoretical respectability with which to conceal the wrongheadedness of their methodology—its fragmentation, its frontal assault character, its failure to provide for natural language use, and its Laputan machinery. These educationists should have known better. It is high time they repudiated "behavioral objectives" and "systems approaches" to the teaching of language skills, as well as the mechanical, dehumanized, and counterproductive teaching approaches that have come to dominate remedial language skills instruction in our schools.

Curricular fragmentation and direct teaching do not work, systems and machines dehumanize and further subvert the learning process, "differentness" labeling is self-fulfilling, and ghetto prejudice devastates absolutely. What, then, can we do? I think our solution begins and ends with people, our educational system's most plentiful resource: people who understand how language skills are learned, people who know that late and slow skills development requires no "remediation" other than patience and forbearance; people who by grace have been freed from bondage to ghetto prejudice; people who view the activity of teaching as a nurturing service rather than the application of technique; people missioned to work one-on-one with less skilled students; people gifted to give the only things a language skills teacher *can* give, an appropriately planned sequence of language activities, a dialogical partnership, corrective feedback, help and encouragement, and constant affirmation.

The answer is really so simple. Eleventh graders who can't write well shouldn't be toiling over punctuation and English usage exercises, or dully poking the keys of a computer terminal, they should be writing poems and essays and stories by the ream, every day, *with a competent writer at their elbow*, helping, teaching, urging, and guiding them. Poor readers in the junior high grades shouldn't be practicing word-attack skills or puzzling over cloze passages displayed on video screens, they should be reading real reading—books, magazines, the daily papers, or each other's essays and reports—*with a competent reader at their elbow*, helping, teaching, urging, and guiding them. For with students far behind their agemates in skills development, the learning process has gotten itself somehow untracked, frustrated, blocked. Only another human being present on the spot can tell what has gone wrong, help the student begin to set it right, and bolster motivation. In this regard, all the fragmenting apparatus of behavioral objectives skills lists laid end to end cannot do what one sensitive and knowledgeable human being can do. They are, in fact, impediments.

Nor do we lack models that we might emulate. There *are* schools in which ghetto prejudice does not exist, where up to half the students are not labeled "mentally handicapped," where all students learn because they are truly expected to learn, where teaching is plain teaching, not "special" or "remedial," where teachers have learned that the most important thing they must do is *wait patiently* while skills develop naturally, and the second most important is to *resist all temptation to stop teaching content* in favor of attempting to teach skills directly. In my own locality, for instance, Marva Collins' highly successful Westside Prep, located in a Chicago black ghetto, a school for children age thirteen and younger who have been branded as failures and defectives by the public schools, shines as a small but brilliant beacon illuminating these simple educational truths. Similarly, the private parochial school in my own neighborhood functions with an administrative bureaucracy of one, houses no remedial programs but does use senior citizens as paraprofessional tutors, and graduates literate eighth graders free of educational stigmata, whose record of success in the large public high school of my city is excellent. There are models of success like these in nearly every community, though their numbers seem small next to the monolith that is public schooling at large.

Ironically, then, it is possible that minimal competency tests may yet perform a valuable function. For if they show that students who fail such tests *keep on* failing them after subsequent skill-drill practice, educators and parents may finally see the light, and throw out the fancy machinery, throw out the one-skill-at-a-time remedial programs, the costly isolation-booth kits and labs and mechanisms that a generation of profit-seeking educational technocrats have foisted upon our schools, throw them out in favor of an investment in human beings teaching human beings, whether peers or adults, professionals or lay persons, by ones and twos and threes, in a fellowship of service that lifts the spirit and uniquely unlocks and draws forth and brings to full flowering the myriad skills of language.

Suggested Readings

Human language and its uses, along with language learning and language teaching, offer boundless opportunities for scholarly study and speculation, from the structural and theoretical to the everyday practical, by specialists working in any number of fields and areas. The following brief list of readings, while in scope as broad as the foregoing chapter, is obviously not exhaustive, nor is it intended for the specialist or scholar. Rather, it aims to provide a modest handful of starting points for the nonspecialist general reader wishing to examine more closely, or pursue a bit further, the general observations on language competence, and the learning and teaching of language skills, that comprise this chapter. For those able to sample only one work on each topic, an asterisk (*) denotes the recommended volume.

Language Competence

In the twentieth century to date, the single most significant contribution to a scientific understanding of the human language faculty is the work of Noam Chomsky, a scholar properly identified as linguist, psychologist, and philosopher. Chomsky's theorizing on the generative-transformational structure of language, properties of universal grammar, and the organic innateness of linguistic structures has been progressing for over twenty years and, one trusts, is far from completed. But as many have learned to their consternation, who have tried to read Chomsky unaided, he does not, naturally enough, write for the general reader. Yet with Chomsky as with other first rank scholars, there is no substitute for meeting a great mind in its own terms and on its own ground. The Lyons booklet, intended for a mass audience, provides a convenient roadmap of that ground, and should be read first. The Allen and van Buren volume arranges and introduces Chomsky's earlier writings for maximum comprehension. Searle's article appraises Chomsky's work from an opposing perspective, that of speech-act theory, arguing that Chomsky's inattention to performance, that is, to principles governing actual communication, reduces the significance of his findings. Chomsky's *Reflections*, a recent and mostly nontechnical volume, addresses the counter-Chomsky issues raised by Searle and others, and contains a great many remarks about language learning and language teaching.

Allen, J. P. B., and van Buren, P., eds. *Chomsky: Selected Readings.* New York: Oxford University Press, 1971.

Chomsky, N. *Reflections on Language.* New York: Pantheon, 1975.

*Lyons, J. *Noam Chomsky.* New York: Viking, 1970.

Searle, J. *Chomsky's Revolution in Linguistics.* New York Review of Books Special Supplement, 1972.

Language Acquisition and Development

Chomsky's theoretical insights almost immediately reorganized psychologists' approaches to the study of language development. The following books, like several others that might just as well be listed here, are intended as texts for introductory collegiate study. Both describe current research methodologies and provide comprehensive bibliographies, and both conclude with material dealing specifically with teaching.

*Cazden, C. B. *Child Language and Education.* New York: Holt, Rinehart and Winston, 1972.

Dale, P. S. *Language Development.* 2nd ed. New York: Holt, Rinehart and Winston, 1976.

Psycholinguistics

Typical of many introductory works on the psychology of language written largely in light of Chomsky's work, the following volume presents contemporary views of how the mind processes language, and of the relation of language to memory, cognition, learning, and meaning.

Brown, R. *Psycholinguistics.* New York: The Free Press, 1970.

Sociolinguistics and Communicative Competence

As implied in the foregoing chapter, a single comprehensive book on this topic remains to be written—indeed, could not have been written as yet, so complex and rapid-growing is the field. The Wolfram and Fasold volume is intended as an introductory textbook on sociolinguistics, and concludes with a chapter on education. While some of the articles in the Cazden-John-Hymes volume are specific in their cultural application, Dell Hymes's "Introduction" will be of importance to all readers. Among the many excellent articles in the Williams volume, William Labov's "The Logic of Non-Standard English" stands out. The Halliday volume describes language development from a perspective different from, but complimentary to, a Chomskyan approach. Halliday calls it a functional, or sociolinguistic, perspective. He describes language development as the learning of the functions language serves, or learning how language means.

*Cazden, C. B.; John, V. P.; and Hymes, D., eds. *The Functions of Language in the Classroom*. New York: Teachers College Press, 1972.

Halliday, M. A. K. *Learning How To Mean*. London: Edward Arnold, 1975.

Williams, F., ed. *Language and Poverty*. Chicago: Markham, 1970.

Wolfram, W., and Fasold, R. W. *The Study of Social Dialects in American English*. Englewood Cliffs, N. J.: Prentice-Hall, 1974.

Reading and Literature

Of all the performance skills of language, none has been longer or more widely studied than reading. Even so, Chomskyan psycholinguistics dramatically altered our conception of the reading process, and rendered obsolete much earlier work. The volumes by Frank Smith provide the most comprehensive introduction available to contemporary thinking and research on reading. As to the appreciation and teaching of literature (poetry, drama, fiction, and other modes of belletristic prose), readers are directed to the Purves-Beach volume, which serves, in effect, as an extended annotated bibliography on this tremendously broad topic.

Purves, A. C., and Beach, R. *Literature and the Reader*. Urbana, Ill.: NCTE, 1972.

Smith, F. *Understanding Reading*. 2nd ed. New York: Holt, Rinehart and Winston, 1978.

*Smith, F. *Psycholinguistics and Reading*. New York: Holt, Rinehart and Winston, 1973.

Discourse Structure

Also in keeping with today's psycholinguistics, the thrust in rhetorical, stylistic, and mode-of-discourse studies is towards greater theoretical precision in defining modes and their organizing structures, as well as fuller empirical confirmation of each mode and substructure identified. Kinneavy's work exemplifies a contemporary taxonomy of whole discourses. Winterowd's volume presents a representative sample of modern rhetorical studies. The work of Britton and his associates reports a long-term project adducing empirical support for their original, multi-dimensioned, and highly illuminating taxonomy of writing modes. Tate's book is perhaps the most exhaustive single-volume bibiliographical survey currently available. De Beaugrande's volume represents the new areas of textlinguistics and network grammars, and draws upon the approach of computer-oriented artificial intelligence study.

*Britton, J., *et al. The Development of Writing Abilities (11-18)*. London: Macmillan Education, 1975.

De Beaugrande, R. *Text, Discourse, and Process: Toward a Multi-Disciplinary Science of Texts*. Norwood, N. J.: Ablex, 1980.

Kinneavy, J. L. *A Theory of Discourse*. Englewood Cliffs, N. J.: Prentice-Hall, 1971.

Tate, G., ed. *Teaching Composition: 10 Bibliographical Essays*. Fort Worth, Tex.: Texas Christian University Press, 1976.

Winterowd, W.R., ed. *Contemporary Rhetoric: A Conceptual Background with Readings*. New York: Harcourt Brace Jovanovich, 1975.

Literacy Teaching

A longstanding though until recently minor theme in twentieth century native-language teaching, in both England and the United States, is that the basic skills of language are best learned, by students of all ages, through practice in the actual use of language, rather than through study and memorization of principles that merely describe such use. Obviously, this is the view presented in the preceding chapter. Until the appearance of Chomsky's theory of language competence, however, teachers were forced to justify such an approach solely on grounds of intuition and personal experience, often laying themselves open to charges of permissiveness and impractical romanticism, which they seldom satisfactorily answered. Since Chomsky, this approach can be justified in terms of systematic linguistic knowledge. Curiously, though, the three volumes listed below pay scant attention to Chomsky's work.

Britton's thinking, for example, is influenced most heavily by the psychologist George Kelly and the literary critic D. W. Harding, while Moffett relies most upon Piaget, George Herbert Mead, and the general semanticists Alfred Korzybski and S. I. Hayakawa. Yet one of the reasons, perhaps now the primary reason, these three remain, after almost ten years, not only credible but the premier one-volume treatments of native English language instruction, is the inference-based but wholly scientific corroboration they have received from Chomsky's theory of language competence.

Britton, J. *Language and Learning.* Penguin, 1970.

Dixon, J. *Growth Through English.* 3rd ed. Reading, England: National Association for the Teaching of English, 1975. (First published in 1967. Available in the United States from the National Council of Teachers of English.)

*Moffett, J. *Teaching the Universe of Discourse.* Boston: Houghton Mifflin, 1968.

Other Readings

Persons wishing to inquire in greater depth into research on the learning and teaching of language skills are directed to current journals of professional organizations such as the National Council of Teachers of English and the International Reading Association, and of discipline-based organizatons of linguists and psychologists, as well as to the Yearbooks of the National Society for the Study of Education, and to the Research Report series of NCTE. These materials are available in any academic library and contain both state-of-the-art information and particular research studies on every aspect of language competence.

Readers with some background in language studies, broadly conceived, may wonder at the absence here of references to scholars and thinkers such as Otto Jespersen and Leonard Bloomfield, Edward Sapir and Ferdinand De Saussure, I. A. Richards and Susanne Langer, Jean Piaget and L. S. Vygotsky, Kenneth Burke and Wayne Booth, Benjamin Lee Whorf, Ludwig Wittgenstein, Jerome Bruner, Rudolf Arnheim, and many others one might mention. The work of these well-known figures has been omitted from this brief list simply because it stands at one remove from the immediate concerns of the present chapter. Clearly, however, it merits the ultimate attention of all people, whether specialists-in-training or interested laypersons, who wish to know, in its variegation and many textures, what modern thinkers make of language—that most marvelous of human organs, the verbally structured, symbolic, abstractive, yet biologically-based system by means of which we cognize, express, communicate, reflect, and dream.

3 Competence in Reading

Alan Purves
University of Illinois at Urbana-Champaign

Reading is a complex mental act in which a person matches what is in his or her head with what he or she perceives on the page in order to get meaning. People's reading of a text is influenced by what they know about the matter in the text, by how they feel about the matter and about the situation in which they are reading (whether they have to take a test on it or remember it for some other purpose). Their reading of a text is also influenced by their level of language skill. Reading skill, therefore, varies from individual to individual and within an individual from situation to situation. One person may be able to get meaning from a physics text but not a poem, another from a novel but not an article about psychology.

How then does one determine the competence of a reader or a group of readers? The criteria of literacy contain so many variables that it is difficult to get reliable estimates of the number of illiterates in this country. If one goes by the written examination for the driver's license, there are few illiterates; if one goes by certain standardized tests, the number increases tenfold or more. Given the graduation requirements of many high schools, one might infer that a competent reader can get meaning from texts of a certain complexity in literature, grammar, rhetoric, mathematics, the natural sciences, the social sciences, and such other areas as home economics, agriculture, and technology. Such a definition begs both the question of "a certain complexity" and the question of subareas within each of the broader subject-areas.

Recently, states and municipalities that have mandated tests of minimal competence have referred to something called "functional literacy" and have defined it in terms of "real-life" texts: directions, contracts, want-ads, and the like. Such a definition adds to the burden of the teacher without diminishing the obligation to help students read the other kinds of texts we have listed. The definition has also served to demean the function of the schools by defining "functional" in such a way as to imply that schools have little, if anything, to do with educating people to take an active role in a complex technological society.

Neither the critics nor the supporters of the schools have a satisfactory answer to two very practical questions: 1) What kinds of texts dealing with what sorts of topics can a "competent" reader read with understanding? 2) What is the best means of assessing a student's competence in reading? The first question clearly relates to the curriculum; the second question relates to testing and test construction but also to the definition of reading skill developed in chapter 2.

What Can a Competent Reader Read?

This question can be broken down into a number of subquestions. What words should a competent reader know? A basic list of 5,000? 10,000? What contexts and what kinds of sentence structures should a reader be able to read? Simple sentences on directions or complex sentences on legal contracts? Logical, narrative, or other contexts? What kinds of topics should a reader be able to read about? Just everyday affairs or all the topics in the New York Times? What kinds of intentions should a reader be able to infer? What a writer wants the reader to think, to feel, to do? The questions immediately complicate the seemingly simple problem of measuring competence in reading. To come up with answers to these questions one may either await the results of a vast program of research that may never be completed or cut through the Gordian knot and arbitrarily make decisions. Obviously, the second choice appeals to those who recognize the need for action—after all, this is what teachers and administrators have done for centuries.

Nevertheless, some of the fruits of research are useful. There are counts of frequently used words, counts of typical sentence patterns, and determinations of the major types of writing.[1] There are also studies of what people do when they read.[2] All of these may help those who must cut the Gordian knot.

To take the matter of words, first, those who have established word counts and studied language have identified a number of words as essential to communication, words like *if, not, on, under, before, after.* These words signal fundamental relationships in time, space, and logic. Then there are the commonly used words of everyday life—*walk, sit, table, chair, sheet, toaster, exit, smoking, loitering, paper.* Where life is more complex so must be the language that reflects it. Thus, what was once technical vocabulary may become common as, for example, have *L.E.D., four-function, microwave.* One has to determine which of these more technical words is important to the functioning life of our citizens; at this point one must become arbitrary and select, say, the words of finance, of automobiles, of home appliances, of law, medicine, and political science. To create a vocabulary test without some sort of context runs the risk of being out of date as well as the risk of measuring only a minor aspect of reading. Virtually always we don't read words but words in sentences, paragraphs, contexts; a vocabulary test is not a test of reading, although it is a test of knowledge.

The discussion of words leads inevitably to a discussion of topics. What kinds of things should an educated citizen be able to read about? Certainly those matters which directly relate to survival—but what are those matters? The threats to survival vary immensely. There are varieties of physical danger, of economic danger, of psychological danger. It would seem important, therefore, for a competent reader to be able to read about a great variety of topics. How can reasonable limits be placed on the variety of topics? Certain ways of setting those limits exist: The topic might be a specialized one, such as meteorology—an important topic for citizens associated with the food industry, and who is not?—but one might limit the topic to what is important for the lay reader. Such a limit might exclude writing on the physics of weather, and at the same time might exclude certain technical terms like *troposphere.* Another way of setting those limits is by assuming that certain topics affect only specialized groups; in medicine, heart disease and cancer affect large segments of the population, but Tay-Sachs disease affects only a minor segment. Thus, a pamphlet on hypertension ought to be comprehensible to competent readers while a pamphlet on Tay-Sachs may not be.

Such rules of limits are, of course, subject to complications, but certainly their use may help to exclude esoteric topics from reading tests. In traditional tests, passages on such topics serve to set an upper limit that distinguishes the very best kind of reader, one who can read almost any journal or encyclopedia article. Tests of minimal competence do not need to serve this function; they seek to establish what everyone can do, not to distinguish varying levels of competence. These tests are not designed to spread students over a normal curve, but to create a cut-off point below which fall students who need additional help.

The very mention of vocabulary and topics in reading tests raises the issue of the whole relationship of reading and general knowledge. One can well argue that in order to comprehend a passage—not simply to pronounce the words—a person must already know something about the topic. I can "read" a textbook in Boolean algebra in the same way that I can "read" a text in Greek: I can sound out the words. But I cannot read either text in the sense of understanding what they are about.

We do not enter the reading act totally ignorant. To take an example from one of the recent competence tests:

> Read this statement:
>> Women should have the right to be educated to their full potential along with men.
>
> If a person expressed this view, which ideas below would he or she most likely believe?
> 1. A woman's place is in the home.
> 2. Women should refuse to do any homework.
> 3. If women do the same work as men, they should receive equal pay.
> 4. Women should make all of the important world decisions.
> 5. Women and men should share household tasks.
> 6. It was a mistake to give women the right to vote.
>
> (A) numbers 1 and 6
> (B) numbers 2 and 4
> (C) numbers 3 and 5
> (D) numbers 4 and 5
>
> ("High School Reading Proficiency Examination," 1974, in NASSP, 1976)

To answer this relatively simple question, a student needs to know some of the premises of women's rights, as well as the extreme feminist and anti-feminist positions. Such knowledge is independent of any vocabulary or reasoning prowess, though both are important for getting the right answer.

A test of reading comprehension is perforce a test of general knowledge. Testmakers must determine what kinds of general knowledge will insure passing the test. Given the world of mass media and vast television watching, children's general knowledge may be broader now than at any other time in society's history. Even a passage like the one on women's rights may be within the children's ken. Since no formulas for determining the breadth of general knowledge exist, the common sense of both the testmaker and the group legislating a competency test must set the limits for the test. Too narrow a band of vocabulary and topics is as great a disservice to schools and students as would be too broad a band; the former trivializes human knowledge, the latter asks the impossible of the general citizen.

Contexts and Structures in Reading Tests

Words are not used in isolation but in relation to each other. When people read, they tend not to read words but larger units of meaning. These units are organized by syntax as well as by a variety of other devices (paragraph relationships, logical relationships, metaphoric relationships, and other relationships which allow words and ideas to be juxtaposed to one another and to be repeated). At times these relationships are signaled in the language; at times we have to infer them.

A writer may put down:

> We ate lunch and then went to the park. John stopped to talk to us.

In the first sentence the *and* signals the relationship between two events; the *to* signals the relationship between an action and a location. There is no such signal between the two sentences. We infer that John talked to us in the park. That kind of inference is fairly easy, as is the inference that enables us to connect two frames in a comic strip.

Many more difficult inferences are called for in the following passage from the Sunday supplement, *Family Weekly*, 1977:

> Just after dawn in Taos, N. M., a virgin snowfall is tested by a lone skier. He zips along the natural slopes engraving the Sangre de Cristo ranges, slowing now and then to savor the crispness and silence of the forest. Later that morning, he joins other skiers at the lodge, sipping steaming hot chocolate and planning the day's instruction logs. After lunch, Tony Rousselot is back on the slopes, a fulfilled and happy man in love with his work and his environment.
>
> Only six years ago, Rousselot was a New York stockbroker, keeping pace with the dynamics of urban life. He had success but had to pay a price—tension, high prices, high taxes, a hectic lifestyle for himself and his family. He was beginning to wonder whether it was all worth it. With some savings, courage, family support and a love of skiing as his backup, Rousselot moved west to Taos and began a new career as a ski instructor, sidelining in horticulture in the off-season.
>
> A FAIRY TALE? NOT QUITE. Rousselot is just another example from the swelling ranks of middle-aged men who are successfully changing their careers in "midstream."

The events in the first paragraph are connected by words of time; the events in the second paragraph are connected to the first by "six years ago." But the second paragraph does not indicate how Rousselot decided to change his life totally. We are told he wonders; then we are told he moved. We infer that a great deal happened between these two sentences. We also have to infer in the next paragraph that the change is a valued change, one everybody would like—or that a lot of people would like. There are some cues —*fairy tale, successfully*—but they, themselves, need a lot of explanation that the writer does not give. To say this is not to blame the writer for writing badly; the passage is quite clearly and interestly written. But the reader has to do some work.

So does the reader of these directions on a box of chocolate pudding:

> Empty contents into saucepan. Add 3 cups milk gradually, stirring until smooth. Stir over medium heat until mixture comes to a full boil. Pour into serving dishes. Chill.

In this example, the reader has to supply those words that indicate sequence—*and, then, next, second*—as well as the ideas that the milk goes into the saucepan and that the serving dishes are to be chilled, not the saucepan. It helps if the reader knows something about cooking. When one tests reading comprehension, then, one tests the inference-making power, the power to connect words, phrases, clauses, sentences, paragraphs and the reader's previous knowledge in order to make meaning.

Another kind of inference a reader makes is almost a precondition of reading. In most situations, as we said at the beginning of this chapter, the reader approaches a text with some idea of what it is—whether it is a story or a recipe, for example. We expect a story to have characters, a plot, and a setting; a recipe to list ingredients; a commercial to praise the product. Few who pick up this book do so with the expectation that they are going to be reading about mathematics or ancient history or that they are going to read a poem. With a general idea in mind, readers also have expectations about the structure and content of the text, which the text either satisfies or denies.

But can one list all of the kinds of structures that a competent reader can read? Is there any way of classifying them in order even to begin to think about a test or a curriculum? One can establish a set of categories of relationships between ideas—and therefore between words—that might serve as a rough guide:

Relationships in time
Relationships in space
Logical relationships
    additive (and)
    negative (but, or)
    conditional (if-then)
    comparative
    contrastive
Associational relationships

Whether such relationships are explicit or implicit might form the basis for determining the difficulty of a passage. But such a measure is crude at best because relationships can change within even so "simple" a piece of writing as a recipe, which may seem to follow a temporal order but have a variety of logical relationships— *and, but, if-then*—embedded in it. Common sense and careful scrutiny of the written text are usually adequate for identifying what relationships are stated and what implied. Certainly it is sensible to exclude from tests passages with those relationships that research indicates are most difficult: complex shifts in time, conditionals, and highly allusive associations like those found in some modern fiction.

A particular form of context, implicit in the foregoing examples of inference-making, is syntax. Some writing is made up of relatively simple syntactic constructions (for example, the pudding recipe where, even though the sentences have no subjects, they contain a few phrases or subordinate clauses). Most writing is more complex than that, as the example from *Family Weekly* illustrates. A sentence like

> He zips along the natural slopes engraving the Sangre de Cristo ranges, slowing now and then to savor the crispness and silence of the forest.

is made up of a number of constituent "sentences" combined into a single complicated sentence. This process of combining is natural in speech as linguists have shown (Chomsky, 1969; Loban, 1976; Strickland, 1962); uncombining them or at least understanding them is a natural aspect of listening. Reading them also seems a natural process easily acquired in the process of learning to read, but there can be problems (Stotsky, 1975). Some sentences can be extremely complex and even a mature reader will have problems unraveling them. Whether these sentences should be included in a competence test is dubious, although the following sentence from

a Master Charge statement represents what any credit buyer should
have to read, and understand.

> The balance on which the FINANCE CHARGE (if any) is com-
> puted is the Average Daily Balance, determined as follows: (i) the
> balance on the first day of any monthly billing period is the a-
> mount shown as "Previous Balance" on the reverse side hereof
> (less any FINANCE CHARGE included therein); (ii) this amount
> is also the balance on each succeeding day in the billing period
> until a cash advance is accepted by Issuer or a payment or credit
> is received by Issuer or an adjustment is made on the account at
> which time such cash advance, payment or credit, or adjustment
> will be reflected by an appropriate change in the balance for that
> day and all succeeding days; (iii) the sum of the balances of each
> day in the billing period divided by number of days in the billing
> period yields the Average Daily Balance.

Since the variety of syntactic structures presented the reader in
everyday life ranges from the Master Charge information to the
pudding directions, it would seem that a test of competence in
reading should include this variety.

Intentions and Purposes of Writing

A reader comes to the text with expectations about purpose as
well as content and structure. The three examples of everyday
writing which have so far appeared represent three writers' efforts
to inform their readers—about how to do something, about how
something has been done, and about a person and his career. A
great deal of the writing concerns itself with informing, but by no
means all. In the same *Family Weekly* these four pieces of writing
occur:

1. Here's where you buy those fun-loving
   ### GRASSHOPPERS
   Sofwear has them—an exciting variety for all your casual clothes
   and activities. You'll love their soft comfort and superb fit!
   ### FAWN—$10.95
   Canvas uppers. Rope-trimmed crepe soles. Adjustable ties.

2. *NEEDLECRAFT/By Rosalyn Abrevaya*
   With one easy stitch, you can create a stunning rug and pillows
   that will adorn any room in your house.
   LATCH-HOOKING: IT'S EASY AND A LOT OF FUN
   WOODLAND SCENE RUG KIT
   This versatile art-on-the-floor rug creation is a pretty decoration
   in any room. Dramatically portraying a forest at sunset, it's worked

in rich shades of pumpkin, white, canary, mahogany and green. The convenient kit includes the design, printed on 3.75 mesh-cotton-rug canvas, precut acrylic rug yarns and complete instruction. The finished size: 27" round.

SUNFLOWER AND STRAWBERRY PILLOW KITS

Cheer up any corner of a sofa or bench with one or a pair of these brilliantly stitched pillows. Sold in separate kits, each design, printed in color on 3.75 mesh-cotton-rug canvas, comes with precut acrylic rug yarns and complete instructions. The finished size of each pillow is 13" x 13".

TO ORDER KITS ILLUSTRATED ABOVE, USE COUPON BELOW. ALLOW 4 TO 6 WEEKS FOR DELIVERY.

3. The goose was a loner, without friend or foe. At last, taking pity on him, the central geese committee began to tout the gaggle about his hidden virtues, and the loner was soon accepted. The moral of this is that what's proper for the goose is propaganda.

Teena Smith

4. OBSERVATIONS

VICTORY AT SEA. When companies bid on offshore tracts with oil and gas potential, both big and small firms have a good shot at the action. In a Gulf of Mexico lease sale last autumn, for example, competition was fierce. Of the 43 blocks on which bids were accepted, 27 went to independent companies and seven to independents and majors bidding jointly. (And the federal government got $375 million in lease bonuses.) All told, since 1967, smaller firms have shared in 80 percent of the winning bids in all federal lease sales. You might remember that next time somebody spouts off about big oil companies driving out smaller ones.

STUMBLING OVER THE WORDING. Wisconsin's *Blue Book*, an official state directory, says members of the Citizens Advisory Council on Alcoholism are "appointed by the governor for staggered three-year terms." We think that's a sobering thought.

STRANGER IN A STRANGE LAND. The "Mobil Showcase" TV series on great adventures, TEN WHO DARED, turns next to Charles Doughty who, in the late 1870s, became the first Christian Englishman to live among the Bedouins in the Arabian desert without denying his faith. Mary Kingsley, featured the following week, showed another kind of determination. When both her parents died, she decided to carry out her father's work in natural history. She traveled among the Fang people of West Africa in 1893, financing her expedition by selling goods along the way. You'll remember both exploits for a long time. Check your local listings for time and station.

DRAMA TO KEEP. The stories of Doughty, Miss Kingsley, and many others are told in the 336-page book TEN WHO DARED. With a preface by Anthony Quinn, narrator of the series, the colorful picture-filled volume will take you on a journey through time from the 15th to the 20th century. You can obtain a copy by sending a check or money order for $14.95, plus applicable state and local taxes, to: TEN WHO DARED, P. O. Box 1934, Kansas City, Missouri 64140.

MOBIL
Observations, Box A, Mobil Corporation, 150 East 42 Street
New York, New York 10017

The first of these is quite obviously an advertisement. The second one seems to inform, but proves to be aimed at persuading the reader to buy some patterns and materials. The third one is intended simply to amuse the reader with its play on words. What of the fourth? It provides information, it tells a joke, but it is also—as we see by the end—an advertisement paid for by a company.

In one Sunday supplement, then, we find a range of writer's intentions. Some of them are fairly obvious; but some are quite complex, if not subtle. The range of possible intentions has been discussed by a number of scholars (Moffett, 1968; Britton, 1975; Kinneavy, 1971) and is summarized in chapter 2, but one can adapt the scheme of purposes proposed by ancient rhetoricians: to amuse, to inform, to persuade.

One of the tasks of the reader is to make the determination of intention; to do so helps the reader decide how to act. If a reader thought that the passage on needlecraft were meant to inform, that reader would emerge from the reading ignorant of how to do such needlecraft. If a reader of the Mobil advertisement thought the passage were meant simply to amuse, that reader would be considered ignorant. To test the comprehension of a reader is to find out whether that reader can see the purpose of a piece of writing.

Beyond finding out the purpose, the reader must also determine the relationship between purpose and effect (what John Mellon calls "critical" reading). Did the joke amuse me? Did I feel about Mobil Oil the way I think they wanted me to? If the reader of the Mobil advertisement thinks that the company is a monster rather than a complex of concerned individuals, the ad writer has failed or the reader has failed. Similarly, if, after reading thus far into this chapter a reader believes I am still making the testing of reading an amusingly simple task even after I have thrown in complication after complication, then somehow I have failed or the reader has failed. To be sure other factors enter in. Some readers may know of my previous writings; some readers may have been influenced by some previous experience with Mobil Oil, so that the effect is not solely the result of the writing. Looking at effect is important in the testing of comprehension because, by determining the relationship between intention and effect, one reassesses the intention of the writer. Just as a test of comprehension is a test of general knowledge, so is a test on the effect and intention a test of a reader's predispositions and attitudes, because the effect is in part shaped by the reader, who modifies what is read by filtering it through a set of assumptions and beliefs.

One way of dealing with this problem is to measure not only the reader's perception of intent, but the reader's perception of tone. This shifts the question from the idiosyncratic to the general, from "Were you amused?" to "Do you think people were supposed to be amused?" Research has shown that there may be quite individual responses—perceptions, feelings, attitudes—to a piece of writing, but at the same time there are certain shared perceptions (Richards, 1929; Purves, 1973; Holland, 1975; Hirsch, 1976). These shared perceptions can be thought of as the *meaning*, and the particular or individual understanding as the *significance*.

A recent newspaper article outlines the problem:

> "Rocky planned his escape. The lock that held him was strong, but he thought he could break it. The situation was becoming frustrating; the pressure had been grinding on him for too long. He was being ridden unmercifully. Rocky was getting angry now. He felt he was ready to make his move."
>
> A prisoner planning a jail break or a wrestler struggling to break a hold? The interpretation depends as much on the knowledge the reader brings to the passage as on the information he finds there, according to Prof. Diane Schallert, a visiting faculty member in the department of educational psychology at the University of Illinois. . . .
>
> "What you comprehend when you read depends on your knowledge of the world," she said. "It is the sum of what you bring to the text and the text itself."
>
> The passage above was shown to wrestlers in a gym class, and most of them gave it a wrestling slant, Ms. Schallert said. The same passage was shown to a group of music students, and many of them read it as a jail break.
>
> It is one of a series of passages constructed for experiments on how a person's background affects his understanding and memory of what he reads.
>
> [They] devised a second paragraph which was not ambiguous. It described a home and its contents in a straightforward way.
>
> Readers were asked to look at the passage either from the perspective of a home buyer or from that of a burglar, and they were tested on what they remembered.
>
> "The person reading as a burglar might remember that there was a coin collection mentioned, while the home buyer would be more likely to remember that there were cracks in the plaster," Ms. Schallert said.

> But although the passage was not artificial, the assigned per-
> spectives were, because the readers were not really home buyers
> or burglars, she said. (Champaign-Urbana *News Gazette*, March 18,
> 1977)

A reading test needs to be a test of meaning, not of significance, of
the fact that Rocky is trying to escape, not as to whether one sus-
pects the situation is a jail or a wrestling arena. A good part of
schooling in reading is devoted to the separation of the two and
of practice in the task of determining meaning. In a test situation,
some students will probably answer questions in terms of significance. Few readers can be so totally objective as the test situation
demands, yet the test must seek to deal with the shared understanding—that to which all must agree, which is the meaning.

A further problem arises. Often a reading test includes a question that seems to be one of meaning, but which is really one of
significance. For example consider this item from the Illinois Inventory of Educational Progress, Grade 11, 1976:

> Read the following paragraph and answer the questions on the
> next page.
>
> Any attempt to label an entire generation is unrewarding, and yet
> the generation which went through the last war, or at least could
> get a drink easily once it was over, seems to possess a uniform,
> general quality which demands an adjective. It was Jack Kerouac,
> the author of a fine, neglected novel, "The Town and The City,"
> who finally came up with it. It was several years ago, when the
> face was harder to recognize, but he had a sharp sympathetic eye,
> and one day he said, "You know, this is really a BEAT generation."
> The origins of the word "beat" are obscure but the meaning is
> only too clear to most Americans. More than mere weariness, it
> implies the feeling of having been used, of being raw. It involves a
> sort of nakedness of mind, and, ultimately, of soul, a feeling of
> being reduced to the bedrock of consciousness. In short, it means
> being undramatically pushed up against the wall of oneself. A man
> is beat whenever he goes for broke and wagers the sum of his re-
> sources on a single number; and the young generation has done
> that continually from early youth.
>
> A. What is the MAIN point of the paragraph?
>   1. The beat generation
>   2. The labeling of a past generation
>   3. The definition of the word "beat"
>   4. I don't know.

In this item, the testmaker has assumed that all readers can agree
to a single *main* point. But the "correct" answer is debatable simply because each option is so brief and none indicates the whole
paragraph's meaning. Each option is a reader's significance—an as-

pect of the paragraph that stands out to one reader or another. There are no "correct" answers to questions of significance, nor any wrong ones either; 1, 2, 3, and 4 are equally "correct" significances.

Towards a Definition of Competence in Reading

So far we have seen that the competent reader has a fairly large vocabulary; a working knowledge of a variety of phenomena in the world; a capacity to deal with a variety of syntactic constructions —both to supply connections and to disentangle complexities; and a capacity to determine meaning, purpose, and intended tone and to separate these from personal significance. We have seen, too, that a competent reader approaches a text with a set of preconceptions and a sense of the context in which reading occurs. In general, one doesn't just read; one has a purpose for one's reading and one reads for many purposes.

Furthermore, a competent reader is flexible or fluent as well as precise. In school, one reads in a variety of subjects to understand them. In the workaday world, one is confronted with a lot of reading—instructions, commands, warnings, pleas—from the moment one gets up to the moment one goes to bed. Many readers "filter" out some of this print; they do not notice words like "Exit," phrases like "Close cover before striking," or whole advertisements or pieces of information such as the name of the manufacturer on a milk carton. Some of that writing seems almost as if it was not intended to be read by everyone. Nonetheless, competent readers seem able to adjust to this plethora of words and to separate the consequential from the inconsequential; more importantly they can read all of this variety if they have to.

Competent readers also have to read a great deal of incompetent writing. Writers—even good writers—do not always make everything easy for the reader; usually they assume their readers are competent enough to follow their meaning. On the back of most airplane seats, facing the passenger in the seat behind are the words, *Use Bottom Cushion for Flotation*. What a curious expression that is! It uses a large word for a short phrase (to float); it is virtually contextless; and it does not indicate when or how. The printed instructions in the seat pocket are not much more helpful.

> The seat cushion of each passenger seat is an approved flotation device and may be used in the event a ditching operation should become necessary.

One wonders why the writer did not say what a ditching operation is (probably so as not to alarm the passenger). As Joseph Conrad noted, "I write; let others learn to read." Such being the way of the world, readers have to be able to do more inferring than writers perhaps intended; amazingly, great numbers of readers do it fairly well and uncomplainingly.

A competent reader must, therefore, perform a number of cognitive tasks in a variety of situations on a variety of ambiguous pieces of writing. At the end of high school, a vast majority of students achieve this remarkable prowess just as twelve years earlier they were well on their way to achieving prowess in speaking and listening.

The role of the school in developing competent readers is varied. At first, the school shows children that the marks on paper have meaning; and it shows them how to interpret the marks. But that is only the first step. The main role of the school in developing competence is two-fold. First, it provides a broad variety of things to be read (stories, problems in mathematics, scientific descriptions, poems, biographies, political documents, and on and on). As has been pointed out in chapter 2, sometimes schools do not so provide and thus cheat the student. Equally important, in school the student is made aware of certain aspects of a text. A teacher will call attention to words, to syntax, to organization, to tone, or to intent and will show the student how the writer uses these to affect the reader. This task is a large instructional job, one that many teachers and critics of the school fail to appreciate. Learning to pay attention to the constituents of texts and to draw inferences from them requires a great deal of instructional time and effort. At the very least, therefore, a test of competence in reading should not cheapen the achievement of students. Nor should it be limited to only one or a few of the activities that indicate competence in reading.

The foregoing discussion suggests that, to be valid, a measure of competence in reading must be constructed under the following constraints:

> Understanding of words in context and of whole passages must be viewed in realistic terms which consider the broad range of topics and contexts that represent the real-life concerns of people. Such competence cannot be limited to mere survival skills nor should it be conceived of in terms of an encyclopedic knowledge.

The kinds of passages selected must represent the variety of logical and associational relationships between ideas and the variety of intentions that exist in everyday reading.

The criterion of competence must be the reader's ability to perceive the shared meaning of the passage, not another reader's personal significance.

How Can Competence in Reading Best Be Measured?

It is not the purpose of this chapter to review all the myriad tests in reading, yet notice should be given to some of the major types of measures. These would include the "conventional" passage accompanied by items, the cloze, and the direct assessment. One might add the vocabulary test and other measures used for some of the subskills of reading (e.g., letter discrimination). A vocabulary test score correlates very highly with a reading test score; but the vocabulary test alone is not a sufficient measure of competence because it ignores the importance of contexts both to the meaning of a word and to the process of comprehension.

Passages with questions have served as the staple of reading tests for several decades. The passages are usually informational prose selected from textbooks, encyclopedias, newspapers, and the like, and they are usually long enough to provide a context. The number of questions may vary, and the type of question may also vary. The following is a fairly typical example:

Top Insurance Problem

Detroit—A man of 21 is at or near his physical peak, his coordination may never be better, and his senses are at their sharpest.

Despite this, when a young unmarried male buys a car and applies for insurance, he will be asked to pay about 2 3/4 times the base rate. If he is married or only drives the family car part time, he must pay 1 3/4 times the base rate. And even then, many companies aren't eager for his business. Why? The insurance people say they'll probably lose money on the policy despite the much higher rate.

His particular age group (unmarried male under 25) is more accident-prone than any other. As yet, young women drivers are not penalized by high insurance rates, mainly because they are outnumbered by the men. But one insurance executive says, "We are making a serious study of the situation. It certainly may become necessary to charge them more, too."

Men and women under 25 make up only 18.4 percent of all licensed drivers. But they are involved in 28 percent of all vehicle accidents and in more than 28 percent of all fatal vehicle accidents. Motor vehicle accidents are the leading cause of death for both males and females from 15 to 24. And one of 17 persons in this age group gets injured in a car every year.

Can the number of accidents on our highways be reduced? Insurance companies are searching vigorously for some new answers to this problem, other than raising rates to everyone. One suggestion is to give financial support to driver education programs in high schools.

KEY: On your answer sheet, blacken the circle containing the letter

    A if the idea stated in the test is an AGREEMENT with the contents of the reading passage;

    D if the idea stated in the test item is in DISAGREEMENT with the contents of the reading passage;

    N if the idea in the test item is NEITHER STATED NOR SUGGESTED in the reading passage.

151. Auto insurance base rates will increase 1 1/2 percent during the coming year.

152. Young married men pay lower insurance rates than young bachelors.

153. More people under 25 drive sports cars than do members of any other age group.

154. High insurance rates are directly related to the high accident rate in the under 25 age bracket.

155. Most of the injuries suffered by young people in auto accidents could be prevented by use of seat belts.

156. Insurance companies have decided not to increase insurance rates for young women drivers.

157. Young people under 25 drive more miles than older persons.

158. Driver education programs in high schools may help reduce the number of vehicle accidents.

(California Test Bureau *Proficiency and Review, Series II,* Form G)

This form of test seems to be more popular than the familiar four-choice reading test selection exemplified previously. In general, the items are unambiguous, although there are some problems in distinguishing the A and D choices from the N choice. In items 156 and 157, both D and N choices have some merit; in item 158 both A and N choices have merit. All three of these statements are related by implication to the text, and the reader must decide whether or not the inference is justified. "It may become necessary to charge [women] more, too." The companies have not decided either way, but for the time being they are operating on a decision not to raise the rates. Since there are fewer drivers under twenty-five than over; it is highly probable that they drive *fewer* miles than older ones. Although insurance companies are contemplating shifting resources to driver's education programs, no proof that such programs would reduce accidents is presented. One would be hard pressed to say whether these three items tap issues of meaning or of significance; certainly the last two come close to dealing with significance.

These items are limited in that they do not tap all of the student's reading skills; sensitivity to language, structure, tone, and intention, in particular, is ignored. These items also illustrate many of the problems of reading comprehension testing. Clearly unambiguous items dealing with meaning are extremely difficult to write. Most tests of this type can be faulted in the way that these items have been: they are not strictly objective and they do not allow for legitimate variance in comprehension.

A fairly recent rival to the multiple-choice test is the cloze test (Bormuth, 1975). The cloze procedure takes a passage and deletes every fifth (or tenth, or some other ordinal) word. The student is asked to supply the word or to select from a number of options the best word. The cloze procedure is based on the principle that words exist in context: the student must read the whole passage in order to make a selection. If one were to take one of the passages cited before and make a cloze test of it, the test might be something like:

> Just after dawn in Taos, N. M., a virgin _____ is tested by a _____ skier. He zips along _____ natural slopes engraving the Sangre de Cristo _____, slowing now and then _____ savor the crispness and _____ of the forest. Later _____ morning, he joins other _____ at the lodge, sipping _____ hot chocolate and planning the _____ instruction logs. After _____, Tony Rousselot is back _____ the slopes, a fulfilled _____ happy man in love _____ his work and his environment.

(I have not been exact in deleting every fifth word, in order to avoid proper names.) The test might ask the student to supply the words or to select from three or four options, such as for the first, a) thunderstorm, b) snowfall, c) skipole. The former method can be scored by whether the student chooses the exact word or by whether the student chooses an appropriate word. Obviously, the second scoring system is more satisfactory because an exact match of the writer's language is not reasonable in a passage like this.

The multiple-choice version of the cloze test avoids this problem but does raise another one: that of providing distractors that are meaningful without being acceptable alternatives. For "sipping

_____ hot chocolate" options like *creamy* or *tasty* would not be appropriate distractors because they could make sense. Even if the distractors make little sense when they are placed in the slot, the multiple-choice cloze test does seem to require the student to read the test and make sense of it.

One variation of the multiple-choice version is a cloze test prepared for the State of New York (Board of Regents, 1979). The test has a series of passages graded by vocabulary and claims to be able to determine the reading proficiency of a student by how far along in the test a student can get.

The Arctic is very far north. It is a cold land. It is icy. It is snowy. Winter is long. Winter is hard. Some plants can grow there. But nothing grows tall. Flowers are tiny. Grasses are low. Even the trees are ___1___. They grow lying down on the ground. They can't grow tall. It is too cold.

1 a) wet   b) short
  c) dead   d) gray
        e) bare

Eskimos live in the Arctic. They know how to dress. They wear warm jackets and pants. These are made from animal skins. The fur is worn next to the body. They wear boots made from seal skins. These ___2___ are important. They keep the Eskimo snug. They keep him dry.

2 a) clothes   b) journeys
  c) lamps   d) jobs
        e) homes

In the fall, the sun rises later each day. It sets earlier. Then the sun does not rise at all. It is dark all the time. There is hardly any ___3___. This is the Arctic winter. It is cold. It is dark. It is hard to hunt. So the Eskimo must be ready. He must hunt before winter comes. He must find food. He must put it away. He must ___4___ as much as he can. Then he will have food in winter.

3 a) wind   b) water
  c) light   d) soil
        e) industry

4 a) sleep   b) save
  c) move   d) breathe
        e) drink

An indispensable element in the development of telephony was the continual improvement of telephone station instruments, those operating units located at the client's premises. Modern units normally consist of a transmitter,

receiver, and transformer. They
also contain a bell or equivalent
summoning device, a mechanism
for controlling the unit's connection to the client's line, and various associated items, like dials. All
of these ___78___ have changed
over the years. The transmitter,
especially, has undergone enor-
mous refinement during the last
century.

78 a) parts   b) costs
c) services   d) models
e) routes

Bell's original electromagnetic
transmitter functioned likewise
as receiver, the same instrument
being held alternately to mouth
and ear. But having to ___79___
the instrument this way was
inconvenient. Suggestions understandably emerged for mounting
the transmitter and receiver onto a
a common handle, thereby creating
what are now known as handsets.
Transmitter and receiver were, in
fact, later ___80___ this way.
Combination handsets were produced for commercial utilization
late in the nineteenth century,
but prospects for their acceptance
were uncertain as the initial quality
of transmissions with the handsets
was disappointing. But ___81___
transmissions followed. With
adequately high transmission
standards attained, acceptance of
handsets was virtually assured.

79 a) store   b) use
c) test   d) strip
e) clean

80 a) grounded   b) marked
c) covered   d) priced
e) coupled

81 a) shorter   b) fewer
c) better   d) faster
e) cheaper

This format seems relatively efficacious, although one should question the notion of grading a text simply by vocabulary.

Supplying words in context obviously forms a strong index of
the ability to make meaning, but there are other aspects of meaning
that elude the cloze procedure: in particular, tone and intention.
They can be dealt with by the procedure, but such tests are much
more difficult to construct validly than are tests which simply ask
the individual to determine the tone and intention of a passage.
The cloze procedure when applied to a passage of complex tone
seems inadequate. Take the example of the previous passage:

... slowing down and then to _____ the crispness and _____
of the forest.

For the first blank, one might offer *savor*, *taste*, and *appreciate*. Why is *savor* the best word? Probably because it catches the overtones of the other two options. To note the appropriateness of this choice requires a fair amount of sophistication on the part of the reader and places the reader in the writer's shoes. The other two words catch the meaning but not the tone or intention; they are not clearly wrong, but they are not the best. A supremely competent reader might choose "savor," but one might be asking too much of all readers to demand high performance on this task.

All in all, the cloze procedure suffices as a measure of meaning, but as a measure of the apprehension of tone and intention, it is simply too tricky, both for the testmaker and the testtaker. The discernment of the tone or intention in actual writing is better measured when the student must consider how a passage is to be received rather than how it might be constructed. Test items that use actual samples of writing and ask the reader what the tone or intention might be seem to approximate the reading task more closely than would a cloze version.

But determinations of tone and intention are difficult; there seems always to be room for doubt as to the precise intention of an author or the precise tone. While the importance of measuring a reader's ability to infer tone or intention cannot be gainsaid, such measurement cannot be of the "guess what the test writer is thinking of" variety too often typical of multiple-choice tests. The reader must be able to make an appropriate and approximate inference. Short answers rather than multiple-choice questioning provide one solution, but if multiple-choice testing seems required, one way of handling it is the following (Cooper, 1973):

> Sample selection A:
>
>> Hats off!
>> Along the street there comes
>> A blare of bugles, a ruffle of drums,
>> A flash of color beneath the sky.
>> Hats off!
>> The flag is passing by
>>> from "The Flag Goes By"
>>> by Henry Holcomb Bennett
>
> SE 1. The poet's attitude toward the flag is one of
>> (a) indifference
>> (b) respect
>> (c) pride
>> (d) perplexity
>
> SE 1. <u>b or c</u>

SE 2. Which one of the following statements best supports your answer to Sample Exercise 1?

    (a) Because the day is warm, the poet suggests that people remove their hats.

    (b) The speaker finds the colors in the flag worth talking about.

    (c) Removing one's hat gives the people behind him a better view of the parade.

    (d) The command to remove one's hat when the flag goes by is a gesture of patriotism.

SE 2.   d

The attitude of the speaker toward the flag may be described as one of respect, or pride, or patriotic feeling, or love. These qualities differ in degree so that to prove that one is a better description than the others is virtually impossible. And just as there is a variety of qualities that describe the speaker's attitude, there are also many qualities that do not define his attitude. Indifference, perplexity, amusement are among those which do not. In the first question of each set, because of the variety of possible appropriate answers, we offer two options that are appropriate, and ask the student to choose one that seems to him *more* appropriate. Although each teacher or student might prefer a different option or some reformulation, we trust that the options offered are acceptable answers and the first question will help teachers find out which students have difficulty finding the range of acceptable answers.

Another way of measuring the comprehension of complex nonliteral texts has been suggested by Paul Diederich, who asserts that reading comprehension, the process of finding meaning, is "broader, more inferential, more between-the-lines than the literal translation, the who-did-what that is the staple item in reading comprehension tasks." He suggests short quotations rather than whole passages, quotations that are complete in themselves and that contain a variety of uses of language, literal and nonliteral, and a variety of tones and intentions (Diederich, 1965).

Directions: On the answer sheet, put an X through the letter of the best of the three explanations of each quotation. For example:

0. We have met the enemy, and they are ours.

    A. We have fought a battle, and we won.

    B. We found the "enemy" but they turned out to be our own troops.

    C. We are their enemies, and they are ours.

The answer sheet would be marked as follows: 0. ⨉ B C because A is the best of the three explanations of this quotation.

You must not expect the best explanation to say exactly what you think the author meant. It need be only a bit closer to this mean-

ing than the other two explanations. Do not make any marks on
this copy of the test.

---

1. The story of any man's real experience finds its startling parallel in that of every one of us.
   A. Truth is stranger than fiction.
   B. Whenever we hear what really happened to someone else, it is surprising to find that something like it has happened to us.
   C. Every person has interesting experiences that would make a good story if he only knew how to write about them.

2. A woman would be more charming if we could fall into her arms without falling into her hands.
   A. Life would be more pleasant if we could go straight to our goal and not run into the obstacles that confront us every day.
   B. A woman would be more desirable if she could be admired without being possessed.
   C. Women would be more charming if we could love them without being dominated by them.

3. The thing generally raised on city land is taxes.
   A. The only thing that grows on the land in cities is the amount of tax you have to pay.
   B. Nothing is grown in cities because their taxes are too high.
   C. It is too crowded in the city to raise any animals or crops.

One advantage of these quotations is that they are complete unto themselves, although some might argue that they are too brief. They are, but in their brevity they contain a number of problems of tone, feeling, intention, as well as meaning. Certainly, their variety, the fact that a test can contain several disparate brief texts, and the fact that the question gets to the main point of comprehension—determining the central thrust of the utterance, all recommend this test design.

The measure of intention might use a variety of passages such as those given above from the *Family Weekly*. Students would be asked to say what the intention is or to match passage with intention. The passages should range from the relatively straightforward —a hard-sell advertisement or a joke or a warning—to the complex like the Mobil ad or even the arguments for and against Proposition 6, which seek to inform and to persuade. The gradation might well approximate what appears in a newspaper, from report to advertisement to feature to institutional advertisement, for a newspaper is a microcosm of most writing situations.

Most of these measures, however, do not fully describe what a competent reader does. One aspect of competence is the subsequent behavior of the reader. How does one measure this sort of competence? You can't have recipes and ingredients or poison bottles in a testing situation—or can you? To some extent one can, or at least one can devise some sort of simulation. To my knowledge it has not been done in any test of competence, although some tests like driver's examinations have used versions of such a simulation. The test might have at its simplest level three labels— one for iodine, one for aspirin, one for lemon juice—and the reader would be asked which one is the label for something you should not swallow. Each label would contain not simply the article's name, but such information as "Poison—not to be taken internally," "Take two with a glass of water," "Add to tea or mix with sugar and water for a satisfying drink." A more complex version of this measure might have three descriptions of a person or a house and ask the student to match the correct one with a photograph. Even more complex might be the instructions to assemble a Tinkertoy and the student would be given the pieces. Correct assembly means that the student has read the instructions (of course, in this case, the student must have some manual dexterity). One test (NASSP, 1976) uses this format:

> Follow the directions below to design a border. Use scratch paper to draw the border.
> (1) You will use squares, circles, and triangles to make your border.
> (2) Draw five squares, four circles, and three triangles in a straight line.
> (3) Erase every third figure and replace it with a circle.
> (4) Starting with the second figure in your line, erase it and every second figure from then on.
> (5) Put a triangle in the first two empty spaces.
> (6) Put a square in the next empty space.
> (7) Put a circle in the next three empty spaces.
> (8) Erase all but the first eight figures.
>
> Which border looks like yours?
> (A) □ ○ ○ △ □ □ ○ △
> (B) ○ □ △ △ □ □ □ ○ □
> (C) □ △ ○ △ □ □ ○ ○
> (D) △ □ ○ ○ □ △ △ □

It seems possible to test by a direct measure most of the meaningful aspects of reading.[3] Such a measure might contain passages of varying complexity. Complexity in this area is, as we have seen, not easily determined, but in addition to using vocabulary, one might use syntax as a dimension of complexity. One might begin with simple sentences, and then add connectives of addition, negation, and conditionality. The border design question might then read something like:

> Using squares, circles, and triangles, first draw five squares, four circles, and three triangles in a straight line, but then put circles in for every third figure. Next after erasing every second figure, replace the first two with triangles, the next with a square, and the last three with circles. If you erase all but the first eight figures, what would you have as your border?

Further complications could be added until the testmaker has approached bureaucratese.

Another criticism of tests of meaning apprehension is that although they follow the Diederich format even for problems of figurative language, ellipsis, and the like, they don't deal with the reading of books. In one instance, a California test (California State Board of Education, 1976) had three columns of prose followed by three items, each of which referred to single sentences in the text. Some would deem this format a waste of time, since in most passages of expository prose the main point is given in a brief introductory or concluding section, while the body elaborates the main point with exemplifications. A more complex piece of writing —like a book—might resist the single summary of meaning that this kind of test calls for. Certainly this whole chapter that you are reading does so. It could be summarized: competence in reading can be measured with complications; but such a summary seems a little bald.

One solution to this quandary lies in the use of nonexpository prose, fiction, perhaps, or even poetry, both of which may be fairly lengthy and complex, but which can only be summarized from a reading of the whole. One way of measurement would be to give a story in full and then give a set of synopses, all but one of which omit a crucial element of the story and add something not in the original. For example, a partial synopsis of "Snow White" might read:

> A princess is put out to die by her wicked stepmother but she is saved and finds seven dwarves with whom she lives happily. After a hundred years she marries a handsome prince.

This synopsis omits the poisoned apple, the death of the stepmother, and adds a false time period. Another might omit the dwarves. Synopsis or precis might be used with other kinds of writing as well. The importance of adding as well as deleting comes from the need to force the student to look at the original rather than simply to choose the longest synopsis.

In this section, we have reviewed many of the different types of measures of competence in reading. One we have omitted is one frequently used, the essay question on material read, but as John Mellon has pointed out, such a measure is best seen as an index of writing rather than of reading. From this review one may conclude that most of the present tests are inadequate and that a great deal of developmental work must be done. In fact, the various criticisms of our educational system and its effectiveness in teaching people to read should be discounted because most of the tests are highly imperfect measures. They represent inadequate sampling of kinds of material, of aspects of reading, and of purposes of reading. In general, teachers in whatever subject who see students in a variety of reading situations are probably better judges of reading competence than is any test. Certainly, their cummulative judgment should be respected. Unfortunately, however, teachers are often discounted and they deprecate their own ability to judge students; it remains necessary, therefore, to try to design the best possible test of competence in reading.

A Possible Test of Competence in Reading

The discussion of competence in reading and of the variety of means of measuring that competence leads to a consideration of specifications for a test of competence in reading:

Understanding of words in context

Determination of meaning of a larger passage

Determination of the intention of a writer

Determination of the tone of a passage

While one could follow the type of test procedure of standardized reading tests and use lengthy passages with questions covering each of these four abilities, it would seem advisable to have separate tests for each (Bloom, Hastings, and Madaus, 1971). The test of words in context might be a cloze test; that of meaning of a larger passage might be a test like the Diederich example with several short quotations supplemented by one or two passages a paragraph or two in length; that of intention might be a direct measure such as the matching of picture to description as in the NASSP test; and the measure of tone might be one like that in Cooper's *Responding* test series. The Diederich example might also be seen as a measure of tone and intention, and could supplement the others suggested.

This format of a test separates the measures into discrete parts.

This is preferable, I would suggest, to a "comprehensive" reading test like that used in most standardized test formats with one passage followed by questions on all these aspects. The problem with the standardized test is that it does not clearly indicate the areas that are being tested or provide adequate safeguards for test construction. Students can miss several questions on reading words in context but correctly answer the questions on meaning. Can the student "read" the passage? Yes. But which of the questions in a standardized reading test is most clearly an index of a student's ability to read that text, of a student's competence? Because of the difficulty of answering that question, I would prefer the test to be divided by the abilities measured rather than by an arbitrary number of passages.

If one adopts such a four-part testing format, the question then remains as to how lengthy each part should be. How many words does a reader have to insert in a cloze test to demonstrate competence? How many topics? In a standardized test format one can create a fairly reliable test with twenty questions or so, but reliability in a competence test is not the same as reliability as we normally think of it. The test is designed to produce a simple distinction—between those who have attained a level of competence and those who have not; a standardized test seeks to discriminate various levels of performance, and so seeks to separate students as much as possible with some very easy questions, some very difficult questions, and some in between. One cannot readily answer the question of length. The New York test is but one example, a lengthy cloze test using graded passages so as to determine the approximate level of proficiency of a student from Grade 2 to Grade 12.[4]

Each of the types of measures except the second, that dealing with whole meaning, is capable of being graded as to difficulty or complexity; even the second could be graded according to the number of elements or the complexity of elements, although as yet we do not know precisely what, beyond vocabulary and syntax, determines the complexity of a piece of writing. In each case, however, it would be possible to fashion a test—based on research or a best guess—that contains items of increasing difficulty. But so doing raises a next question, and a most crucial one. How far along each continuum must a student read in order to be certified as competent? The answer to this question does not come easily. Functional literacy has been defined in terms of achieving a certain grade level or of performing certain tasks. The first of these seems arbitrary, based as it is only on vocabulary; the second seems overly specific. In terms of the tests that have been advanced here, one could either set arbitrary standards or use the empirical approach to find out what is reasonable for most students to be able to do when they are in ninth or tenth grade. This approach appears to resemble the norm-referenced test but differs in that one must not simply accept the average performance of a group of students but weigh this against one's subjective sense of what is reasonable and practical. One must arrive at a compromise between the normative and the reasonable.

We have reached the point then, when we can reaffirm that the competence of a student as a reader could be determined with a four part test: understanding words in context, determining the meaning of the whole, determining the intention, and determining the tone. But we do not know at what level a reader is competent. Years ago, I. A. Richards found that Cambridge University students were incompetent at *his* level (Richards, 1929). Others have come to similar conclusions; I am incompetent vis-à-vis Bertrand Russell, fairly competent vis-à-vis Shakespeare, quite competent vis-à-vis Mark Twain. One is never a wholly competent reader; but a good reader keeps wrestling with words, meaning, tone, and intention. Perhaps, after all, a competent reader is one who is willing to try to understand.

With having uttered that platitude, I realize the practical necessity of dealing with the problems of schools and with the pressure to sort students. Certainly we have no adequate definition of "minimum competence" or "functional literacy" to which all can agree. I think that the solution of the National Assessment—of giving a sample task and the percentage of children who can perform that task—is preferable to a label like *competent* or *illiterate.* But that, too, begs the question. If we can come up with four graded subtests, as I think we can, then I think a school system could set reasonable levels of expected achievement at specific grade levels. Should students not perform at those levels, the school could then check the result with the observation of the teacher. Should those two results match, some kind of program—perhaps a broad reading program, perhaps some form of specific remediation—might follow. In general, it is better to describe the level of competence a student has attained than to set an arbitrary level for all students. Competence in reading knows no minima or maxima. Students and teachers should be made aware of this situation, and that can best be achieved by not setting a fixed and unworldly level of competence.

Notes

1. There have been several studies in this century of frequently used words (Thorndike and Lorge, 1944; Carroll, 1971). From these studies, one can determine an appropriate list of words for a passage and problems in a reading test. Similarly, there have been studies of the commonly used syntactic patterns of students of different age and abilities (Strickland, 1962; Hunt, 1966; Loban, 1976); and of major rhetorical types (Moffett, 1968; Britton, 1975; Kinneavy, 1971). From these studies, one can systematically predict what kinds of writing using what kinds of sentences and what kinds of words might make an effective test of reading. As the ensuing discussion shows, however, this approach may be misguided because creating texts for competence tests may prove artificial and insufficient to the variety of real-life reading an individual must face. Far better to use the research as a guide to selecting a variety of "real" pieces of writing.

2. These are summarized in Purves and Beach, 1973.

3. This type of measure might also be used for other types of reading, such as the reading of maps, graphs, and charts. Some might consider skill with these materials is properly the domain of mathematics, geography, or other social sciences rather than of reading. It is difficult to make a decision as to the appropriate area of measurement. But whether they belong in a test of competence in reading or in mathematics or in geography is less important than the fact that they should indeed be measured, for a competent citizen must maneuver in the world of written language and the worlds of other symbol systems. Maps, timetables, calorie charts, diagrams: all have to be read by most people in this country, not simply by the specialist.

4. During the course of this chapter, I have cited test items from a variety of sources. As the reader may have noted, some of these sources are research documents (Diederich, 1965), out-of-print (Cooper, 1973), or state-owned tests (Board of Regents, 1976). A review of currently available commercial tests indicates that there is no one set of available tests that matches the general set of specifications cited in this chapter. A beleagured administrator has two options (perhaps, three): to settle for the single test that seems to fit most of the criteria; to ask staff or an outside consultant to create a test following these specifications; or to use several commercially available tests—or parts of tests—and assemble a jury-rigged test. I suppose the second option is the best; the third is a manageable compromise; the first what most administrators will finally select. If one is going to choose the second option, I would suggest going well beyond the sources listed at the end of this chapter, which are but a sampling. Certainly, one should consult the reports of the National Assessment of Educational Progress.

References

Bloom, B.; Hastings, J. T.; and Madaus, G. *Formative and Summative Evaluation of Student Learning.* New York: McGraw-Hill, 1971.

Board of Regents. *Degrees of Reading Power: Test Form G.* Albany: State of New York, 1976.

Bormuth, J. "Literacy in the Classroom." *Help for the Reading Teacher: New Directions in Research.* Edited by William D. Page. Urbana, Ill.: National Conference on Research in English and ERIC Clearinghouse on Reading and Communication Skills, 1975.

Britton, J.; Burgess, T.; Martin, N.; McLeod, A.; and Rosen, H. *The Development of Writing Abilities (11-18).* London: Macmillan Education, 1975.

California State Department of Education. *California High School Proficiency Examination.* 1976.

Carroll, J. B., and Chall, J. F. *Toward a Literate Society: The Report of the Committee on Reading of the National Academy of Education.* New York: McGraw-Hill, 1975.

Carroll, J. B.; Davies, P.; and Richman, B. *The American Heritage Word Frequency Book.* Boston: Houghton Mifflin, 1971.

Chomsky, C. *The Acquisition of Syntax in Children from 5 to 10.* Cambridge, Mass.: MIT Press, 1969.

Cooper, C. *Responding: Evaluation Sequence.* Boston: Ginn and Co., 1973.

Diederich, P. B. "A Test of Understanding of Quotations." Mimeographed. Princeton, N. J.: Educational Testing Service, 1965.

Family Weekly, 20 February 1977.

Hirsch, E. D. *The Aims of Interpretation.* Chicago: University of Chicago Press, 1976.

Holland, N. *Five Readers Reading.* New Haven, Conn.: Yale University Press, 1975.

Hunt, K. W. *Grammatical Structures Written at Three Grade Levels.* Urbana, Ill.: NCTE, 1966.

Illinois Inventory of Educational Progress, Grade 11. Springfield, Ill.: Office of Education, 1976.

Kinneavy, J. L. *A Theory of Discourse.* Englewood Cliffs, N. J.: Prentice-Hall, 1971.

Loban, W. *Language Development Kindergarten through Grade Twelve.* Urbana, Ill.: NCTE, 1976.

Moffett, J. *Teaching the Universe of Discourse.* Boston: Houghton Mifflin, 1968.

National Association of Secondary School Principals. *Competency Tests and Graduation Requirements.* Boston: NASSP, 1976.

Purves, A. *Literature Education in Ten Countries.* Stockholm: Almqvist and Wiksell, 1973.

Purves, A., and Beach, R. *Literature and the Reader: Research in Response to Literature, Reading Interests and Literature Teaching.* Urbana, Ill.: NCTE, 1973.

Richards, I. A. *Practical Criticism.* New York: Harcourt Brace, 1929.

Smith, F. *Understanding Reading.* New York: Holt, Rinehart and Winston, 1971.

Stotsky, S. L. "Sentence Combining as a Curricular Activity: Its Effect on Written Language Development and Reading Comprehension." *Research in the Teaching of English* 9 (Spring 1975): 30-71.

Strickland, R. G. "The Language of Elementary School Children: Its Relationship to the Language of Reading Textbooks and the Quality of Reading of
Selected Children." *Bulletin of the School of Education, Indiana University*, no. 38, 1962.

Thorndike, E. L., and Lorge, I. *The Teacher's Wordbook of 30,000 Words.*
New York: Columbia University Press, 1944.

4 Defining and Assessing Competence in Writing

Lee Odell
Rensselaer Polytechnic Institute

With reports of the National Assessment of Educational Progress—Writing (NAEP-W) and with extensive media commentary on "Why Johnny Can't Write," the American public has become greatly concerned about students' writing ability. Evidence from NAEP-W and from several other sources has led people to conclude that students are not writing as well as they once did. And a number of experts, legislators, and concerned citizens alike are telling us about the present "crisis" in writing. It does little good to point out that this crisis is not new or to argue that our current understanding of it is derived from questionable data. Nor does it help to tell critics that writing is a complex skill, one that is hard to teach and perhaps even harder to assess adequately. All of these assertions are true. But none of them responds to a growing sense that the public, not to mention our students, deserves a comprehensive assessment of our students' competence as writers.

We can provide such an assessment. Without oversimplifying a very complex activity, we can describe and evaluate our students' writing performance. Later in this chapter, I suggest specific ways we might go about this. But these suggestions will make sense only if we can agree upon answers to four questions:

1. What are our purposes in evaluating students' writing? What do we hope to learn as a result of an evaluation?

2. What do we mean by *competence* in writing?

3. What kinds of tasks does *writing* entail?

4. How useful are existing procedures for measuring writing ability?

These questions are so important that I want to consider them in some detail before making specific recommendations about evaluation.

Purposes for Evaluation

One way to understand our purposes for evaluating students' writing is to decide what sort of questions we want our evaluation to let us answer. One basic question is this: *How well are students doing in their writing?* Which students are the best writers and which are the poorest? Which students are at least minimally competent and which are not? A different sort of questions is this: *What do students need to do in order to become better writers?* What weaknesses must they overcome? Are there any strengths that teachers might help students build upon?

One can answer the first sort of question without answering the second. When teachers are trying to assign final grades or when colleges are trying to identify students who are most likely to do well in their college English courses, the first set of questions may be the more important; one may only need to know which students are the most skillful writers, which are somewhat less skillful, and so on. But for our purposes as teachers, categorizing or grading students is not enough. If we are to help all students write as well as they can—and if we are to provide adequate remedial work for noncompetent writers—we must have answers to the second kind of question. In other words, we must have a useful diagnosis as well as a judgment about students' relative skill as writers. Accomplishing both of these purposes depends in large part upon a set of assumptions about what it means to be a competent writer.

Competence in Writing

John Mellon's discussion of "language performance skills" should forewarn us that defining competence in writing will not be a simple task. Unquestionably, our definition will have to make it clear that we value what Mellon calls "mastery of the rules of writing." That is, we will consider students "competent" writers only if they can observe certain conventions of spelling, punctuation, and capitalization. But competence, even "minimal competence,"[1] entails something more than mastery of conventions. A student's response to the following assignment should help illustrate my point.[2]

> *Assignment:*
> Some high school students have proposed converting an old house into a recreation center where young people might drop in evenings for talk and relaxation. Some local residents oppose the plan on the grounds that the center would depress property values in

the neighborhood and attract undesirable types. A public hearing has been called. Write a brief speech that you would make supporting or opposing the plan. Remember to take only ONE point of view. Organize your arguments carefully and be as convincing as possible.

Student essay:
I feel that the young adults of our community need this old house to be converted into a recreational center. Everyone, especially young adolescents, need a place of belonging. If you as a community would help to make their dream come true you would be saving yourself a lot of trouble in the future. You would not have the worry of your young children hanging out at street corners drinking or down at some store causing trouble. Maybe even getting involved with drugs. You would always know where they were with proper guidance over them.

This essay contains relatively few glaring errors. There is only one sentence fragment, only one instance in which a comma is incorrectly omitted, only one instance in which a verb (*need*) does not agree in number with its subject (*everyone*). From the standpoint of correctness, the student's writing performance might be judged minimally competent. But given the assigned audience and purpose, it is hard to argue that the content of the paper would let us call her performance competent or even minimally competent. The writer simply ignores the issue of property values, an issue that the assignment indicates is important to those people in her audience who oppose the recreation center. And even supporters of the project might feel uncomfortable with the superficiality of her arguments. She makes several hypothetical statements (if the center is built, teenagers' dreams will "come true"; if there is a teen center, teenagers will stop hanging out on corners; if teenagers are at the center, they will not have access to alcohol or drugs), any of which is open to serious question. It appears that the student has not thought in any detail about her own assertions or about the objections that opponents might raise. Presumably, we want this student (and any other) to be able to use writing as something more than a way to demonstrate that she has mastered the conventions of standard written English. If our evaluation (and consequently our teaching) focuses on only this student's mastery of these conventions, there is a great danger of misleading ourselves and the student about her competence as a writer.

If we are to avoid misjudging our students' writing, our notion of competence must encompass the range of skills suggested in Mellon's discussion of "communicative skills": "fluencies—lexical, syntactic, creative," "discourse skills," and "critical and appreciational skills." In order to make this array of skills more manageable for both teachers and evaluators, I want to subsume them under two general headings: discovering ideas and making appropriate choices.

Competence: Discovering What One Wishes to Say

For most of this century, the teaching and assessment of writing have been almost exclusively concerned with what classical rhetoric referred to as Arrangement and Style. The most widely-used texts (Warriner and Griffith, 1957, for example) are preoccupied with helping writers see how to organize their writing, how to observe certain conventions of formal written English, and how to avoid certain logical fallacies in presenting their ideas. But as several writers have pointed out, these texts omit any reference to what classical rhetoric calls Invention, the process by which writers discover what they wish to say.

Reasons for this omission are understandable. The process of discovery is essentially a thinking process; if we equate thinking with "logic," it is easy to assume that logic, which is taught in other disciplines such as philosophy or mathematics, is not the province of English. If we accept this line of reasoning, we may define competence in writing as skill in organizing and expressing ideas, information, or feelings. But this definition is too limited. It ignores Mellon's point that the "discovery of content" is one of "the most important keys to success in writing."

The importance of the process of discovery becomes especially apparent when we encounter students who just can't think of anything to write about. Before these students can proofread their work to eliminate errors in spelling and grammar, they have to have something to say. They have to explore their subject matter in order to determine what they think or feel about the issue at hand. In this respect, our students have something in common with highly skilled writers. A novelist and Pulitzer Prize winning journalist, Donald Murray (1978) notes that, "As writers, we are drawn forward to see what argument comes forth in our essays, to find out if hero becomes victim in our novels, to discover the reason for an historic event in our biographies, to experience the image which makes a blurred snapshot in our memory come clear in our poems." The important thing about Murray's claim—and the evidence he uses to support it—is that he is not just talking about "creative" or "literary" writing. For writers of poetry, argumentation, biography, and fiction, the predicament is the same: writing is not always a matter of putting on paper a set of stock responses or prefabricated ideas that exist independently of the writer. Ordinarily, writing a letter, a memo, or a report requires writers to give some conscious thought to what they wish to say; they must come to a conclusion about the topic at hand.

It is very likely that this process of discovery will vary from writer to writer or even from task to task. Certainly, no two writers proceed in exactly the same way. Yet from reading observations of children's writing and professional writers' accounts of their own composing, and from thinking carefully about what we do when we ourselves set out to write, we can identify a few of the types of behaviors writers engage in as they attempt to discover what they wish to say.

For many writers, the process of discovery begins not with writing but with talk. When asked to write an essay in response to the question "What do you do when you write a paper?" a graduate student reported that usually "I talk about my papers with my roommate. We hassle, harangue, clarify, and beat each other with the data until we put the puzzle together." Although this student was talking about a very specialized kind of writing, her experience may not be unique. I suspect that many business letters and memos contain ideas that began to form as the result of a phone call or a casual office conversation. I know that assertions in scholarly articles may arise from an argument with a colleague or an attempt to explain some idea to students.

For certain young children the process of discovery may include drawing as well as talking. Donald Graves (1975) reports that some children sketch out pictures of the action they are describing; as they add details to their pictures, they also add these details to their written narrative. Writing prompts their drawing, and their drawing enriches their writing.

For other writers, the discovery process begins with what Peter Elbow (1973) calls "free-writing," in effect an attempt to brainstorm on paper. Elbow reports that he frequently sits down and writes as fast as he can for a brief period of time—perhaps as little as ten or fifteen minutes—making no attempt to edit or even to decide in advance what point he wishes to make. Frequently, Elbow finds that he can look back at this free writing and find useful insights that he would not have anticipated when he sat down to write.

Since the process of discovery may vary widely, we might not want to assess this performance directly. Certainly, it seems unfair to insist that all students must have mastered a single discovery procedure. But the role of discovery in the process of composition has an important bearing on the limitations of existing procedures for measuring writing ability and provides the key to improving the ways we evaluate students' competence as writers.

Competence: Making Appropriate Choices

Running throughout Mellon's discussions of communicative skills, discourse skills, and critical and appreciational skills is the assumption that writers' choices (of language, syntax, content) must be guided by their awareness of the audience and purpose for which they are writing. Too often, students demonstrate by default the importance of this awareness. Unexplained assertions, unclear transitions, puzzling terms that have a special meaning known only to the writer—all these problems may suggest that students are producing what Linda Flower (1979) calls "writer-based prose" rather than "reader-based prose." Students incorrectly assume that the audience knows what the writer knows; students fail to consider the needs, interests, and knowledge of the persons who will read their text.

A more positive and sophisticated illustration of Mellon's assumption can be developed from the following short passages. The first is a statement found on the cover page of a "Price List Bulletin" issued by a publisher of standardized tests.

> The prices listed herein conform with the provisions of the Executive Order stabilizing prices, wages and rents announced on August 15, 1971, and subsequent implementing orders and directives. Planned price adjustments for 1971 have been temporarily suspended.

The second piece of writing, cited by Kenneth Macrorie (1970), is an excerpt from a college teacher's dittoed note to students who were planning to go on a college-sponsored bus trip to a Chicago art museum.

> Trippers will meet at 7:15 (Kalamazoo time) in front of the Union. The bus will leave promptly at 7:30 a.m. There will be no watering stops between Kalamazoo and Chicago, so I strongly recommend that you all eat something vaguely resembling breakfast before we start—something substantial and comforting like a Hershey bar. . . . After lunch everyone is on his own in the museum. Museum fatigue is a very real phenomenon and I caution you to use some restraint in your viewing, taking the 20th century first and whatever else you can manage after that.

Putting aside the question of which of these is the better (or whether either piece is "good" writing), these two pieces show the sort of choices writers may need to make in conveying their basic message. The importance of these choices becomes especially clear if we consider alternative ways of expressing these two messages. For example, the first passage *could* have been written like this:

> We'd planned to raise our prices for next year, but we can't. At least not right now. The feds won't let us. So the prices of things listed in this brochure go along with the executive order issued a while back that puts a lid on prices and so forth. Maybe you should try to take advantage of the situation and place your orders now for materials you'll need next year.

The second passage *could* have been written like this:

> Participation in the proposed tour of the Chicago museum of art is contingent upon participants' arriving at the Western Michigan State University Union prior to the scheduled departure time of 7:15 a.m. (Eastern Standard Time). Participants should be advised that there will be no stops between the point of departure and the scheduled arrival in Chicago. It is recommended, therefore, that participants make adequate preparation for the journey.

In the revision of the first passage, the price list bulletin, sentences are much shorter and are much less complex than in the original. Word choices are more casual (*feds* is more likely to occur in conversation than in writing, whereas a phrase such as *listed herein* is more likely to appear in formal proclamations or official documents), and there are personal references (*you* and *we*) rather than the impersonal abstractions (*Executive Order*) found in the original. In the revision of the second passage, instructions to the college students, the situation is almost reversed. Personal references (to *I* and *we*) have been replaced with impersonal nouns (*participants*), sentences have been made longer and more complex, and the language is less conversational (the colloquial *watering stops* is replaced by *stops*).

In addition to changes in diction and syntax, both revisions also show small but important changes in the content of the original passages. Deleted from the revised memo to college students is a detail (the reference to a Hershey bar as "something vaguely resembling breakfast") that helps create the passage's whimsical, offhand quality, a quality that makes the writer's advice a little less authoritarian, a little less irritating to his audience of late 1960s college students. Included in the revision is information (the full title of the student union) that is totally unnecessary for the audience of the original memo. The revised statement on the price list bulletin adds to its informal, unbusinesslike tone by including gratuitous advice about taking advantage of the price freeze and excluding precise information, found in the original, about the date and title of the federal restriction on price increases.

I assume we can agree that neither of my revisions is an adequate substitute for the original. The college professor apparently wanted to convey some information and also give some advice—no mean trick when dealing with college students. Consequently, the teacher needed to be as engaging and personable as possible. The impersonal bureaucratic voice we hear in my revision would be inappropriate for the intended audience and purpose. By contrast, the writer of the notice on the price bulletin was merely trying to convey information without giving advice or creating any personal bond with his or her audience. Thus, the writer was probably wise to avoid the rather chatty voice and intimacy with the audience implied in my revision. Given their different audiences and purposes, each passage is a creditable, if not superb, piece of writing. Each writer has made choices of diction, syntax, and content that seem appropriate for the intended audience and purpose.

In making this judgment, I am accepting the following assumptions from rhetorical theory and modern communication theory. (1) Writers must know what sort of voice or personality they wish to convey, and they must be clear about their relation to their audience. (2) Writers must also have a good sense of the purpose they wish to accomplish in their writing. (3) An awareness of this complex relationship between voice, audience, and purpose must govern writers' choices of language, sentence structure, and content.

A Definition of Competence

Implicit in my discussions of "discovery" and "appropriate choices" is a definition of competence that is more complicated than that found in many composition texts. Some of the most widely used texts, such as Warriner and Griffith's, equate competence with the ability to follow the practice of "educated people," to observe the conventions of formal written English, to write clearly, correctly, and concisely. This textbook notion of competence is of some use, especially in certain formal situations. But it ignores the fact that in order to write effectively, one must have something to communicate and one must be able to discover what he or she wishes to say. Furthermore, the textbook definition of *competence* does not account for all the choices writers make, even when they are on their very best linguistic behavior. This latter point is demonstrated in the passage from the "Price List Bulletin." The writer refers to "planned price adjustments." Not *price changes* or, heaven forbid, *price increases.* The choice of *adjustment* seems entirely appropriate. Not because the term is more concise or more correct than *changes* or *increases.* And certainly not because it is less ambiguous. (If anything, adjustments is slightly less clear than *increases*; it allows two possibilities—increasing and decreasing—whereas only one action is likely.) The choice of *adjustments* seems appropriate because it maintains a rather dignified tone and has positive connotations that seem unlikely to offend one who reads the price list. After all, when something is "adjusted," it is usually set right, put in proper working order.

Frequently, success in writing hinges on one's ability to make the sort of choice represented by the phrase *price adjustments.* One must be able not simply to make choices that are correct, clear, or concise, but also to make choices that seem likely to achieve a given purpose for a given audience. Consequently, we have to expand the textbook definition of competence. We must redefine competence to mean *the ability to discover what one wishes to say and to convey one's message through language, syntax, and content that are appropriate for one's audience and purpose.*

Different Kinds of Writing Tasks

The importance of being able to make appropriate choices becomes especially clear when we consider some of the changes that have lately taken place in writing instruction. For many years, secondary schools emphasized the writing of narrative and expository essays in which students were to convey information to a single kind of audience, usually a teacher. This emphasis still appears in some schools. But in recent years, many English teachers have expanded the English curriculum to include diverse kinds of writing ranging from dialogue to journals to dramatic dialogues and reportage, as well as formal exposition and narration. Moreover, teachers, many of them influenced by James Moffett (1968), today ask students to write for different kinds of audiences, some of them sympathetic and well known to the writer (a close friend, for example), others relatively distant and not necessarily sympathetic (the editor of a local newspaper, for example; or members of a school board). Teachers also encourage students to write not only to convey information but also to express their own feelings and perceptions or to try to influence someone else's actions or feelings.

Even though rarely reflected in currently used measures of writing ability, these teaching practices are well-founded in theory. The work of Moffett and of James Kinneavy (1971), Walker Gibson (1969), and James Britton (1975) illustrates the great diversity of writing tasks that must be done in the "real" world as well as in the classroom. These theorists do not completely agree as to how we might categorize these tasks, but they do agree on two points: 1) the global term *writing* includes a great many modes (ranging from diary entries and memos to formal reports) and quite diverse purposes and speaker-audience relationships; 2) different modes, audiences and purposes require writers to use various "registers," to choose different organizational strategies, and even to provide different types and amounts of information.

As an illustration of this second point, consider two accounts of the flood that struck Rapid City, South Dakota in 1972. The first is a diary written by a flood victim while she was trapped in the attic of her house during the flood.

> This amazing little book has just survived the flash-flood of June 9, 1972, in Rapid City, South Dakota. I can't believe my senses. I am all muddy, the whole house is muddy, the first floor is still two-thirds full of water. My electric clock is stopped at 10:37 p.m., and I am writing this by candle light. Actually, the flood at its fullest, I guess it's called the crest, lasted from 10:37 'til about 11:00 or 11:15, if I can make an educated guess. It seemed like an eternity. I have never before prayed for my family's and my life.
>
> Maybe I'd better start from the beginning. I can't seem to write quickly enough. Mom, Dad and I golfed this afternoon. As we were finishing, the weather was threatening, everything was very dark and humid. We went home and had dinner. I sewed on my slacks, and I talked Mom into going to the Toby Theater production of *The Last of the Red Hot Lovers*. Well, we got dressed and went out, and it was raining pretty heavily. We had to take umbrellas and water raincoats. I remember that just as we got by Canyon Lake, I commented to Mother that I had never seen such heavy rain in Rapid City and that the streets seemed to be filling up pretty quickly. We were already going through pretty deep puddles, but they were relatively few and far between. We got downtown to the theater and the show had been cancelled, because one of the actors couldn't get in from Rockerville. . . .
>
> [Later that evening, after the writer had discovered that the creek behind her house had risen so much that she and her family could not get out of the house, the diary writer continues.]

We all got into the attic and I listened to the thunder and lightning and water falling on our roof, rushing by our house. . . . We still don't know how many houses besides ours are standing. After sitting up in the attic for awhile, 'til about 11:30 I think, we noticed the water was really going down at quite a fast rate. . . .

Meanwhile, from the glimpses we've seen from flashes of lightning, we are completely surrounded by debris up to maybe ten feet high. It's hard to say. Somebody's roof is on the corner of our house. Dad's Toronado is standing straight up and down on its back end near the front porch. Poor Mom and Dad! I was so proud about their remodeling, and they were so pleased and proud too. Dad has spent a whole month building a huge sundeck on the back of the house. When I say by himself, I mean by himself. He was just sick. . . .

The second account of the flood consists of the first three paragraphs of a *Reader's Digest* article that appeared shortly after the flood.

It was one of the worst flood disasters in our nation's history. Starting early on Friday evening, last June 9, and continuing through most of the night, an unpredicted and unprecedented 10 to 14 inches of rain spilled onto one small area of western South Dakota where normally only 14 inches of rain fall in an entire year. The steep rocky, 3500-to-7000-foot-high Black Hills could not absorb the torrential runoff which picked up battering-ram force as it funneled through narrow canyons and dropped toward the grasslands to the east. Thundering against the back door of Rapid City, a placid community of 43,000 people, the flash flood crumpled a 34-year-old earthen dam and unleashed a rampaging five-foot-high wall of water through the heart of the town, the second-largest in South Dakota.

Before the rains stopped and the flood dissipated early Saturday morning, 237 people had died, five were missing and 5000 had been left homeless in a 30-mile-long, half-mile-wide path of sudden destruction. Dozens of bridges were destroyed, 5000 cars were demolished or damaged, 1200 homes and about 100 business buildings had vanished.

The cause of the black night in the Black Hills was a freakish coincidence of weather conditions. Although the official forecast for the day had been "partly cloudy, with scattered thundershowers, with some possibly reaching severe proportions," there was no evidence to suggest exceptional rainfall. In fact, a local technological institute continued its aerial cloud-seeding experiments throughout the afternoon, in expectation of typical showers (meterologists say these tests had nothing to do with the deluge). But in the late afternoon a strong breeze blowing from the southeast carried an unusually moist supply of air to the eastern side of the Black Hills. Here the steep slopes forced the incoming air upward, causing great amounts of moisture to accumulate over the hills.

Normally, high-level winds would carry much of this moisture
away—but on this day, the upper-level circulation had come to a
near standstill. The damp accumulation hovered, almost motion-
less, and the rains began to fall.

These two pieces of writing are similar in that each recounts
events that took place prior to the flood, and each details the destruction caused by the flood. Yet, clearly the two writing tasks
are different. They are intended to appeal to different audiences
and they try to accomplish different purposes. I have the sense
that the writer of the diary has set out to answer the sort of question a relative or close friend might ask: What was it like to go
through this sort of experience? Consequently, the diary writer
can choose to narrate her own and her family's actions just prior
to the flood. None of these actions pertains directly to the flood,
but all of them (playing golf, sewing slacks) have a familiar, ordinary quality that contrasts effectively with the shock and chaos of
the flood. When the writer describes the flood itself, she does so
from a very limited perspective; she reports only those scattered
details that are briefly illuminated by flashes of lightning. Such
details are fragmented and allow only a small and not necessarily
accurate picture of the flood. But the very fragmentation helps a
reader understand something of how this experience must have felt
to one who was involved in it.

In the second article, the writer is apparently trying to appeal to
an audience that is interested in the nature and extent of the disaster, not simply one person's perceptions. Consequently, the first
few paragraphs try to answer such questions as these: What was so
special about this disaster? How did it come about? Why is it of interest to someone who has no personal involvement with the flood
victims? Details concerning the uniqueness of the flood (it was one
of the worst in the nation's history) help answer the first and third
questions. Information about the progress of the flood waters (beginning in the Black Hills, bursting a dam) and about the unusual
weather conditions that caused the flood help answer the second
question. In providing a comprehensive, accurate answer to the
three questions I have mentioned, the writer had to go well beyond
his personal experience and draw upon a variety of authoritative
sources to convey the extent of the flood and its consequences.

In appealing to their different audiences and trying to accomplish
different purposes, these writers have to answer different questions
and draw upon different sources of information. They are, in short,
doing different writing tasks. We can not judge these tasks by ex-

actly the same criteria. For example, we can expect the magazine article to provide a reliable account of the entire disaster. But we cannot expect this of the diary writer.

On the face of it, I suppose, this line of reasoning must seem obvious enough. But if we accept it, we shall have to make substantial changes in the way we assign and evaluate writing.

Existing Procedures for Measuring Writing Ability

In the previous sections, I have defined competence in writing as the ability (1) to discover what one wishes to say and (2) to choose the appropriate language, sentence structure, organization, and information to achieve a desired purpose with a given audience. Given this definition, I have serious reservations about many existing procedures for assessing writing competence. One type of procedure, the standardized test, is so limited, in some cases so badly conceived, that it cannot provide an adequate picture of students' writing performance. For most purposes, the procedure of collecting a sample of student writing is preferable to the use of a standardized test. Yet even with writing samples serious problems arise.

Standardized tests. Multiple-choice, "objective" tests seem attractive partly because they can be scored quickly and reliably and partly because they have good predictive validity. That is, some makers of standardized tests have been able to show that if students make a relatively high score on a standardized test, they are likely to make a relatively high grade in a subsequent writing course.

One of the chief difficulties with standardized tests is that they may not measure what they claim or appear to measure. For example: McGraw-Hill publishes a test whose title claims that the test measures "language proficiency." The initial sentence on the test booklet makes a more modest claim: "This test is designed to measure your ability to recognize correctly written English." Ability to recognize correctly written English is, at most, one of several skills that make up language proficiency. Yet a close look at items on the test suggests that the test may not even measure this limited skill. Many of the items on one form of the test do not require students to recognize correctly written English. Rather, they ask students to identify an error in written English. Recognizing errors without necessarily being able to correct them seems like such a small part of language proficiency that I might not have mentioned this test at all. But I found it listed in a National Association of Secondary School Principals publication (1976) as an instance of a "writing" test currently in use. Unless readers of the book happened to look closely at the items in the test itself, they could easily conclude that this test was, in fact, a test of writing. Conceivably, a school's assessment of students' writing skill could rest substantially upon students' ability to identify (to *identify*, not to correct) one of three kinds of errors in formal written English.

Another shortcoming of standardized tests is that skills needed to do well on these tests are not the same as skills needed to do well in writing. For example, multiple-choice tests frequently ask students to choose from among several alternatives that someone else has identified. But for writers, the primary problem is not one of choosing from among such a list of alternatives but of generating their own alternatives from which they will choose. In other words, writers must not merely make good choices of language and sentence structures; they must create those choices. Furthermore, once writers have created alternatives, they must decide which alternative is most appropriate for their intended audience and purpose. Standardized tests—at least those I have examined—do not ask students to make such decisions.

One of the more ambitious tests, the Sequential Test of Educational Progress: Writing (STEPW), claims to measure students' ability to choose "a level of usage suitable to purpose and reader; i.e., using the right 'tone' and appropriate diction and employing tact where desirable." Form I B of the STEPW contains a number of items in which students are asked to choose the "best," the most "appropriate," the most "effective" version of a given passage. In all but one of the items, *best, appropriate,* and *effective* appear to mean least ambiguous, most concise, most in keeping with the conventions of standard written English. As I have already suggested, this notion of competence is not comprehensive enough to let us distinguish between writers who are competent (even minimally competent) and those who are not.

Writing samples. The problems I have described thus far are unlikely to occur when we try to measure students' competence by asking for writing samples. Other problems, however, often arise, problems that will affect both students and evaluators. For example, students are sometimes required to complete their writing in a single session which may last no more than twenty minutes. Within this brief writing period, students must:

> Contemplate a topic *to which they have likely given little previous thought*
> Identify their audience and purpose

> Decide upon the rhetorical strategies they will need in order to achieve their purpose with their intended audience
> Write a first draft
> Reconsider and, where necessary, revise that draft
> Edit their draft to make sure it corresponds to the conventions of standard written English.

Quite clearly, some students will be more successful than others in coping with the demands imposed by these conditions. But these conditions hardly seem conducive to writers' doing their best work. Moreover, these circumstances are pointless and arbitrary. They will rarely apply to other writing tasks students do. Even writing essay answers on examinations, students will (presumably) have in their minds specific information on the topic they are writing about and will have given some previous thought to it.

Other problems are likely to arise when we are obliged to create more than one writing task. We may, for example, want to measure students' growth over a semester or year and therefore may need to create two writing tasks, one to use early in the term, one to use at the end. Or, faced with the need to assess the writing of a large and diverse group of students, we may want to allow students some choice as to the topic they will write about. In either of these situations, we must be sure that the alternative tasks are as comparable as possible.

Yet, it is surprisingly easy to create assignments that make substantially different demands. Consider, for example, a writing assessment that lets students choose to write in response to either of these assertions:

> Much of the instruction that goes on in public school classrooms does not adequately prepare students for college.
> There should be a mandatory jail sentence of at least one year for any person convicted of possessing more than three ounces of marijuana.

These assertions seem similar in at least two respects. Both statements invite the request to "agree or disagree with this statement." Moreover, either statement might provoke a strong response from a writer. But the two topics differ in at least one important way. The first raises questions of fact. To express agreement or disagreement, a student would need to recall specific school experiences and determine whether the information/skills/attitudes resulting from those experiences are consistent with the information/skills/attitudes required in college classes. By contrast, the

word *should* in the second assertion raises not only questions of
fact but questions of law and morality.

Classical rhetoric makes the distinction between questions of
fact, definition, and degree. And James Moffett (1968) has made a
strong argument that writing about what might or should happen
is quite a different matter from writing about what has already
happened. All of us know of these distinctions; but frequently we
fail to consider them in assigning topics. Consequently, we undermine at least two of our purposes in evaluating students' writing.
If students are doing substantially different writing tasks, it seems
unfair to rank order their writing; we cannot say that one student
writer is more or less skillful than another unless students are writing about topics that require similar skills. Further, we cannot determine whether student writing is improving if the demands of
the topic we assign early in the term are significantly different
from the demands of a topic we assign late in the term.

Another problem arises when teachers fail to provide information about the audience students are to address or the purpose
they are to accomplish. One response to this criticism is to argue
that we have made purpose reasonably clear when we ask students
to "agree or disagree" or to "explain your point of view and support it with evidence." But these instructions may be less clear
than they seem. Consider the experience Richard Lloyd-Jones
(1977) reports from his work with the National Assessment of
Educational Progress. One of the NAEP assignments asked students
to agree or disagree with the assertion that "A woman's place is in
the home." Perhaps because the topic is so emotion-laden for
many people, students wrote expressive discourse rather than the
persuasive discourse NAEP had expected. That is, they articulated
their own views on the subject, but they rarely tried to enlist their
audience's sympathy, or to establish common ground with someone whose views differed from their own, or to anticipate questions
that might arise from those differences in views. Ultimately, NAEP
decided to consider this task an expressive task and instructed judges
to rate student papers by asking, in effect, two basic questions:
(1) How often do students elaborate upon the reasons they give for
their position? (2) From what sources (personal experience, authority, other) do students derive this elaboration? For an expressive
task—one in which writers simply articulate their own opinion—
these questions (and the criteria they imply) seem appropriate.
But if this were a persuasive task, judges would have to consider
additional questions such as: Does the writer anticipate a reader's

objections? Does the writer choose elaborations that are likely to seem plausible to the reader he or she is addressing?

Purpose, then, is always a factor in writing assessment. If we fail to be explicit about students' rhetorical purpose, we may fail to help them see how they might develop their ideas. And this failure may encourage students to do different types of writing, some of which invite judges to ask one sort of question, some of which invite judges to ask other types of questions.

A similar line of reasoning holds true for *audience*. Theory, research, and our own experience tell us that an understanding of audience is important for a writer. But frequently our practice in assessing writing contradicts or ignores theory, research, and experience. As in the case with *purpose*, we sometimes have our reasons for not indicating the characteristics of the audience students are addressing. Students, we assume, should know that they are writing for English teachers and that they need to accommodate the expectations of that audience. In some respects, this assumption is reasonable. But even in acknowledging this point of view, we must not oversimplify our conception of teachers as an audience. Their values may be more diverse than one might think.

One way to test this speculation is to remember the last time we attended a common paper-grading session, one at which—with no prior training or discussion of criteria—we and our colleagues read and graded a set of essays. In my own experience, comments made at those sessions indicate that people are using different sets of criteria and are attending to different aspects of the writing, some responding to diction and syntax, some to organization, some to what Diederich (1974) refers to as "quality of ideas." Thanks to recent work by Sarah Freedman (1979), we have reason to think that for some readers "quality of ideas" weighs very heavily in the evaluation of a piece of writing. But even here, we may find considerable diversity, especially when we consider the evaluations of teachers in different disciplines. In my school at least, teachers of business courses frequently give students a set of facts about a company and ask students to recommend policies that the company should adopt. In evaluating students' papers, these instructors seem concerned with matters of practicality. Have students identified one or more specific courses of action for the company to follow? Given the information at hand, does it seem likely that the company in question *could* and *would* follow the writer's recommendations? In economics courses, instructors seem most concerned about the accuracy with which students apply economic theory to new sets of data. In at least one political science course, the instructor places great emphasis on the imaginativeness of students' synthesis of materials studied. Practicality, accuracy, imaginativeness: these are not the only criteria by which instructors judge the "quality of ideas" in students' writing. But just these few examples should warn us that even academic audiences may vary quite widely.

Interestingly, some students are sensitive to these variations. It is not unusual to hear students talk about trying to "psych out" a teacher, attempting to figure out what a teacher values and how a student can appeal to the teacher's values. Carried to an extreme, this effort can preclude original thought and honest expression. But at best, this attempt simply reflects assumptions explained early in this chapter: a writer needs to assess the interests, feelings, knowledge of his or her audience and to use that assessment in choosing language, syntax, and content.

It should go without saying that students will vary in their concern with audience and purpose. Some will seem oblivious to these matters, at least in the writing they turn in to teachers. But by creating writing tasks that specify audience and purpose, evaluators may try to accomplish different goals for different groups of people. Students who are aware of the demands of audience and purpose may improve their understanding of the rhetorical problem they must solve in their writing. Evaluators may get a better sense of the criteria that are appropriate for judging a given set of papers. And teachers may have an additional reason for encouraging all student writers to attend to audience and purpose.

Suggestions for Measuring Competence in Writing

In considering specific procedures for evaluating writing, we must remember that students have a right to expect their coursework to prepare them to do well in areas where they will be evaluated. And teachers have an obligation to make sure that students receive this preparation. This combination of expectation and obligation almost guarantees that evaluation will influence teaching procedures and, indeed, the writing curriculum itself. If we adopt evaluation procedures that reflect a trivial or overly simple understanding of *writing*, those evaluation procedures can do a double harm. They can mislead us about students' skill as writers. And they can misdirect the work we do as teachers of writing. Consequently, all the suggestions in the following section are based on one assumption:

our procedures for evaluating writing must be consistent with our best understanding of writing and the teaching of writing.

Obtaining an Adequate Sample of Students' Writing

The task of assessing competence in writing does not begin with our devising useful criteria or reliable scoring procedures. The task begins with our obtaining an adequate sample of students' writing performance. Unless we have given students reasonable opportunity to make their best showing as writers, our judgments about their competence as writers will almost certainly be limited and misleading. To obtain a good sample of their writing performance, we need to:

> Have students write under circumstances that approximate the conditions under which important writing is done
>
> Ask them to do more than one kind of writing; that is, have them write for more than one audience and purpose
>
> Provide them with information about the audience and purpose for which a given piece of writing is intended
>
> Assess the demands of our writing assignments, especially when we create more than one assignment
>
> Base our judgments on an adequate amount of students' writing

Conditions for writing. When most of us write, we usually take time to engage in the process of discovery. This process may have begun well before we actually started to write a draft; it may have begun with our talking with friends or reading about our topic. If the topic seemed especially important to us, we may have revised our initial drafts. Some writing, of course, receives little forethought and no revision. But the more important and complex the writing task, the more likely we are to plan, revise, and polish our writing before exposing it to public scrutiny.

Given our own experience as writers, it should come as no surprise that our students may benefit from being able to write under the same sort of circumstances we usually enjoy. Granted, we must ask students to work under some restrictions. They must meet certain deadlines, and, for various reasons, we may want them to do their writing during classtime. But even with these constraints, we can set up procedures that encourage students to explore their topic, consider their audience and purpose, and revise and edit their work. For example: to prepare her students to do a piece of expressive writing, an eighth grade teacher[4] proceeded as follows. After reading the short story "Flowers for Algernon," the students talked about the "losses" experienced by characters in the story. Students then discussed the kinds of losses they themselves might experience and identified some of the ways (death, moving to a new town, accidentally breaking a prized object) those losses might occur. Finally, each student listed some of the losses he or she had experienced and made notes about the feelings that accompanied those losses. After this activity, the teacher gave the students the following writing assignment. "Think of some loss you have experienced. Tell what you especially remember about what you lost, and how it feels to experience such a loss." To help students understand the purpose for the assignment, the teacher made sure that the class discussion contained a number of references to personal thoughts and feelings (What thoughts were going through the character's mind when he realized he was going to lose his new-found mental ability? How would you have felt in such a situation?). The teacher also stressed the point that students were to write for an interested, sympathetic audience. These procedures enabled her to make it clear to students that their writing must contain more than a recital of objective facts.

To help his students write about the topic *losses*, a twelfth grade teacher[5] spent class time not only on discussion and note-taking, but also on revision. During the class period when students were to revise their first drafts, this teacher instructed students to work in pairs, each partner reading and commenting on the other's writing. Students were allowed to use these comments in revising their papers.

If we allow time for students to engage in the composing process (perhaps one class period for drafting and one period for revising and editing), we can assume that some students will say everything they have to say in a few hastily scribbled sentences. Even among university students, we can be fairly certain that some students will revise much less extensively than will others. (See Richard Beach's study (1976) of the revision strategies of college students.) These students will probably not need all the time we allow for doing a given piece of writing, especially if they have never been taught how to develop their ideas or to revise their writing effectively. But we are not interested solely in these students. We need to assess *all* our students—those who have trouble putting words on paper, those who make substantial changes in their first drafts, and those for whom revising means little more than changing an occasional word. Thus, it seems important to ask students to write under conditions that seem likely to allow all students to do the best work they can.

Kinds of writing to be evaluated. Quite frequently, the evaluation of writing ability is restricted to assessment of students' skill in writing expository essays, especially those with certain formal features: an explicit thesis statement; several paragraphs supporting that thesis, each with its own topic sentence; and a concluding paragraph. One argument in favor of such a restriction is that the overall goal of many school writing programs is to help students learn to write satisfactory exposition and that, consequently, our main concern should be to find out whether students are becoming more skillful in doing this sort of writing.

It is possible to accept this argument and still use the evaluation procedures described in the remainder of this chapter. A good description of students' performance as expository writers is worth having. But there is a strong argument against limiting our evaluation in this way. The ability to do one sort of writing task may not imply equal ability with other kinds of tasks. An evaluation of students' expository essay writing may tell us little about their ability to do other kinds of tasks which are important in students' personal lives and in their careers. Further, we have, at present, no basis for claiming that one kind of writing task is equally important for all students in all schools in all communities. My recommendation, then, is that we need to evaluate several different kinds of writing performance. The exact number and the specific kinds may well vary from school to school, reflecting teachers' best judgment about the needs of a given group of students.

Designing writing assignments. From the earlier discussion of audience and purpose, it should be clear that our assignments must do more than pose what we hope are interesting topics. When they read our assignments, students must be able to see what their purpose is, whether they are to:

> persuade—that is, influence someone else's actions or feelings
>
> inform—that is, simply provide accurate, comprehensive data that readers can use as they see fit
>
> express—that is, articulate their own point of view without trying to influence their readers or without trying to provide objective information

Students will also need to understand their audience. Even if they are writing for a teacher, they must be able to answer such questions as these:[6]

1. How much does my audience know about this subject?
2. What is my reader's attitude toward me? Is he or she sympathetic? Hostile? Interested in my personal feelings or conclusions?
3. Does my reader have values, preconceptions, or feelings that might influence his or her response to the subject or to what I say about the subject?

Our assignments might also indicate whether students' writing should take one of several forms such as the following:

Dialogue	News Report
Journal Entry	Editorial
Monologue	Essay
Letter	Summary
Memo	Short Story

Even though these divisions of purpose, audience, and form are not exhaustive, they suggest a huge number of writing assignments, many more than we would have time and energy to evaluate during a single school year. We will, consequently, have to reduce the number of kinds of assignments as much as possible without giving up information that we consider important. To accomplish this, we will have to decide where our priorities lie. We might, for instance, decide that students at a given grade level should be expected to write effective persuasion. In this case, we might create different writing assignments by asking students to try to persuade different audiences. One task might ask students to influence a close friend's actions.

> Your best friend, who is having a lot of problems at home, has been acting strangely at school—stumbling in the halls, falling asleep in class and getting really bad grades. One day in the restroom, you see him/her taking a drink out of a bottle. You become concerned that your friend may be on the way to becoming a teenage alcoholic. When you tell your friend how worried you are, he/she says "Leave me alone. I don't need your help." It's a tricky situation, but you feel strongly about helping your friend. Write down the advice you would give in order to get your friend straightened out.[7]

Another task might ask students to persuade a more remote audience.

> Imagine that you have just read a letter to the editor of *TV Guide.* The person who wrote the letter complained about all the violence on TV—cop shows, horror movies, even cartoons like Road Runner. He said that these shows are teaching young people how to be violent, and because of this the shows should be taken off the

air. Think about this problem for awhile. Then write your own letter to the editor either agreeing or disagreeing with the man who
wrote the protest letter. As you write, be sure to include as many
sensible reasons as you can think of to support your opinion.

On the other hand, we might take a different approach and decide that we want to know how well students can write for a certain kind of audience—an adult audience, say, one that tends to be
rather tough-minded and skeptical. In this case we would create
different writing tasks by asking students first to try to *persuade*
this audience. (For example: Members of the school board are
trying to decide whether to try to save money by cutting out certain school programs such as music and art or by cutting out extra-
curricular programs such as athletics. Decide which course you feel
the school board should take and write a speech you will deliver at
the next school board meeting. Try to persuade the board to accept
your point of view.) A second kind of task would ask students to
explain a complicated series of events to the same sort of audience.
(For example: When you brought your parents' car home last
night, there was a good-sized dent in the right fender. Explain to
your parents' satisfaction how the dent got there.)

Teachers' awareness of current events and their own students'
interests will probably produce writing tasks that will be more engaging for a given set of students. My concern is to stress two
points. Writing tasks must not only include a topic but also an in-
dication of audience and purpose. Since there are several kinds of
audiences and purposes, which make different demands on writers,
we must specify audiences and purposes that are consistent with
our expectations for our own students. We cannot measure students' performance on all kinds of writing assignments, but we can
assess their skill with those kinds of tasks that seem most important for our students.

Assessing the demands of writing tasks. We cannot guarantee
that all students will perceive a given topic exactly as we do. In a
group of any size, some students will misinterpret our writing assignments; others may approach the task in interesting ways we had
not even considered. But perhaps we can avoid making students'
lives needlessly difficult if we follow several procedures. If in previous years we have made a practice of allowing students to choose
from among several topics, we might review papers from previous
years, asking: Do students consistently choose some topics and ignore others? Do students who choose topic X consistently receive
higher grades than do students who choose topic Y? We might also

compare and contrast some of the most successful papers about two or more different topics. Better yet, we ourselves might try to write on each of these topics. But whether we examine students' writing or our own, we need to ask such questions as these: Do different topics require writers to draw upon different sources of information? Does one topic require writers to be particularly conscious of their own or someone else's assumptions? Does one topic invite chronological development, whereas another requires analogical development? As we answer these questions, we may realize that we must reformulate—and retest—our writing assignments.

Amount of writing to be evaluated. Despite the widespread practice of trying to measure individual students' writing ability by evaluating one piece of writing done under test conditions, we have reason to think that a single piece of writing may not be a reliable sample of an individual's ability. In a study of college freshmen, Gerald L. Kincaid (1953) found that writers' success in doing assigned writing varied from day to day and from topic to topic. Surprisingly enough, this was especially true of the more skillful writers in Kincaid's study. Thus, if we want to make a reliable judgment about an individual writer's ability to perform a certain kind of writing task, we must have at least two pieces of that person's writing. *Note*: If we want to assess a student's ability to perform more than one kind of writing task, we must have at least two samples of the student's writing for *each kind of writing*. Let us assume, for example, that we are interested in evaluating a student's skill with two different kinds of writing: persuading a close, sympathetic audience and explaining a process to a remote, uninformed audience. We would have to examine at least two pieces of writing in which the student tried to persuade the sympathetic audience and at least two pieces of writing in which the student tried to explain something to the remote audience.

Obtaining a valid, reliable sample of an individual student's writing is especially important when we are trying to determine whether or not an individual student has achieved minimal competence as a writer. We may, on the other hand, be less interested in assessing an individual's competence than in determining the average writing ability of a large group of students. We might want to know how well students in, say, the tenth grade are, as a group, able to do a given kind of writing. In this case, one piece of writing from each student would be sufficient. If we want to assess the group's performance with several different kinds of tasks, we must collect a writing sample for each kind of writing we want to evaluate.

Choosing an Appropriate Measure of Writing Competence

There are at least six ways we might measure writing competence:

1. counts of errors or deviations from standard written English
2. analysis of syntactic fluency
3. analysis of coherence
4. general impression scoring
5. analytic scales
6. primary trait scoring

In the light of my earlier definition of *competence*, each of these measures has certain uses, each has certain limitations.

Errors. The phrase *standard written English* refers to correctness in punctuation, capitalization, agreement of subject and verb, and all the other matters we lump together under the terms "mechanics" and "usage." When we evaluate students' mastery of standard written English, we are, in effect, evaluating their ability to edit, to observe a specific set of conventions that are important in many kinds of writing. Even though mastery of these conventions is not the most important aspect of competence in writing, failure to observe these conventions can, nonetheless, detract from the effectiveness of a piece of writing. Consequently, we need to assess students' mastery of these conventions.

In carrying out such an evaluation, our biggest problems will be deciding which conventions we will be concerned with and how we will recognize errors in the use of these conventions. We will need to categorize the errors in our students' work and limit our evaluation to those types of errors (use of commas in place of periods; failure to make subject and verb agree; confusion of *their*, *there*, and *they're*) that seem most important for the students we are concerned with.[8]

As we try to categorize the errors in students' writing, we will need to resolve a surprising number of tricky questions. Must there be a comma after *all* introductory adverbial clauses, even very short ones? (If the answer is *yes*, much of the published writing students see contradicts our answer; news magazines omit commas wherever possible. If the answer is *no*, we must have some consistent way to determine when the omission of a comma is an error.) Shall we mark as incorrect a very common usage such as "none of us *are*"? Shall we record an error if a student writes *longrange* or *long range* rather than *long-range*? If a student fails to use *ed* in forming the past tense of a verb, shall we count that as an error in spelling or an error in verb usage?

Once we have resolved such problems as these, we may take Charles Cooper's suggestion (1975) and simply count the number of errors that appear in two papers (totalling at least 300 words in order to have a reliable sample) from each student. We might be tempted to use a standardized test (such as the TSWE) on the assumption that students might play it safe in their writing and avoid conventions of which they felt uncertain. Certainly, students' performance on one of these tests would give us some idea of students' ability to choose a correct usage when that usage was one of several choices someone else identified for them. But these tests would not tell us whether students could (and would) make proper choices when left to their own devices as writers.

The chief problem with relying exclusively on counting deviations from standard usage has already been pointed out. The ability to avoid certain kinds of errors does not necessarily imply competence in making choices (of diction, syntax, and content) that are appropriate for one's purpose and audience. Consequently, any assessment of students' command of standard written English should not be used as the sole measure of students' writing ability. Rather, this assessment—or, indeed, assessment of syntactic fluency or coherence—should be done in conjunction with an evaluation of the communicative or rhetorical effectiveness of students' writing. (See the discussion of general impression, analytic scale, and primary trait scoring procedures below.)

Syntactic fluency. Thanks to the work of Kellogg Hunt (1965; 1977), Francis Christensen (1967), and John Mellon (1969), we have precise, well-tested procedures for describing sentence structure, and we have a great deal of information about the development of mature syntax, what Mellon calls *syntactic fluency.* We know, for example, that certain syntactic structures that often appear in the writing of twelfth graders rarely appear in the writing of eighth graders. We also know that growth in syntactic fluency is reliably indicated by increases in the average length of a writer's T-units. (A T-unit is one main clause plus any subordinate clauses attached to it. Using the terminology of traditional grammar, we would say that a simple or complex sentence contains one T-unit; a compound or compound-complex sentence contains two or more T-units.) To compute average T-unit length, we may follow Cooper's suggestion (1975) and mark off a total of forty-five T-units in three or more pieces of writing done by a given student. Then we simply count the words in those T-units to get the average or mean T-unit length.[9]

The great advantage of evaluating students' syntactic fluency is that Hunt and others have provided a substantial amount of information about the sort of syntactic structures we may expect of writers at different age levels. There are, however, two reasons to be cautious about relying too heavily on measures of syntactic fluency. For one thing, syntactic fluency is only one aspect of writing competence. Moreover, when Hunt compiled his data on syntax, he did not make any distinctions between different kinds of writing. He did not try to determine whether syntax might vary according to a writer's purpose and audience. Yet recent studies by Cynthia Watson (1979) and Marion Crowhurst and Eugene Piché (1979) show that we might expect to find this variation in writing done by students in high school and college. Consequently, when we assess syntactic fluency, we must consider the type of writing we are dealing with.

Coherence. In evaluating any piece of writing, we may reasonably ask: How coherent is this writing? Has the writer helped me see the relationships among sentences, paragraphs, or larger sections of the writing? When we try to decide how to answer these questions, our experience and intuition tell us that some kinds of writing are likely to seem coherent if they contain details that clearly support the writer's argument or if there are general statements that tell a reader what to expect in a given section of the writing. Other types of writing, personal experience narratives, for example, are likely to seem coherent if they follow a clear chronological sequence or if they contain only those details that are consistent with the mood the writer is trying to create.

To supplement experience and intuition, we can draw upon the work of several scholars. Ross Winterowd (1976), for example, argues that there are seven "coherent relationships beyond the sentence," relationships that can be labeled *coordinate, obversative, causative, conclusive, alternative, inclusive,* and *sequential.* Frequently, although not invariably, these relationships are signaled by explicit transitions. For example, coordinate relationships may be signaled by the presence of words such as *and, furthermore, also*; obversative relationships may be signaled by *but, yet, however,* and others. When these relations are explicit or clearly implicit, a text is likely to seem coherent.

Another[10] likely source of coherence is what M. A. K. Halliday and Ruqaia Hassan (1976) call "cohesive ties," linguistic features which indicate that one sentence or clause is related to another. Although Halladay and Hassan's complete system of analysis is very complex, they have identified five basic types of cohesive ties, which can be illustrated fairly easily.[11]

Reference

I haven't finished grading the essays. *They* have been on my desk for several days.

(By referring to a noun in another clause, the pronoun *they* serves as a cohesive tie between the two clauses.)

Substitution

I have finished grading the first set of essays, but I haven't read the *others*.

(The word *others* links the two clauses by serving as a substitute for the phrase *set of essays*.)

Ellipsis

I have finished grading the first set of essays, but I have not graded the *second*.

(In the second clause, the phrase *set of essays* is omitted and nothing is substituted for it.)

Conjunction

I have graded the first set of essays, *but* I have not graded the others.

(The conjunction *but* indicates an adversative relationship between the two clauses; other conjunctions may indicate an additive relationship (*in addition, moreover*), a causal relationship (*because, consequently*) or a temporal relationship (*first, then, now*).

Lexical Cohesion

I have not finished grading my students' essays. I'm afraid their *papers* will not be as good as I had hoped.

(The repetition of a related word—or in other instances, the same word—makes two clauses cohesive.)

A detailed analysis of cohesion has not as yet been used in a large-scale assessment of writing. However the 1980 reports from the National Assessment of Educational Progress indicate that readers have been able to use the following rubric in assessing cohesion and coherence.

1 = *Little or no evidence of cohesion:* clauses and sentences are not connected beyond pairings.

2 = *Attempts at cohesion:* evidence of gathering details but little or no evidence that these details are meaningfully ordered. Very little would seem lost if the details were rearranged.

3 = *Cohesion:* details are both gathered and ordered. Cohesion does not necessarily lead to coherence, to the successful

binding of parts so that the sense of the whole discourse is greater than the sense of its parts. In pieces of writing that are cohesive rather than coherent, there are large sections of details that cohere but these sections stand apart as sections.

4 = *Coherence:* while there may be a sense of sections within the piece of writing, the sheer number and variety of cohesion strategies bind the details and sections into a wholeness. This sense of wholeness can be achieved by a saturation of syntactic repetition throughout the piece and/or by closure that retrospectively orders the entire piece and/or by general statements that organize the whole piece.

If we want to assess the coherence of students' writing, we might follow the procedure used in the 1980 National Assessment of writing. We would give judges examples of linguistic features that make writing coherent, and we would ask judges to read a number of sample papers, identifying the ways in which these papers demonstrated or lacked coherence. Then we would ask judges to rank papers on a numerical scale, using a scoring rubric similar to the one developed by National Assessment.[12]

It would also be possible to ask judges to make a much more detailed analysis. For example, we might ask judges to determine how often students' writing showed lexical cohesion or how often students expressed or implied one of the seven coherent relationships identified by Winterowd. However, we must remember that different types of writing may display different types of coherence. For instance, Dixie Goswami and I (1980) have discovered that some adult writers use lexical cohesion relatively frequently in one type of formal writing and relatively infrequently in one type of informal writing. Consequently, we must not assume that any one characteristic of coherence or cohesion is equally important for all types of writing.

General impression, analytic scale, and primary trait scoring. In addition to considering errors, syntactic fluency, and coherence, we must make some judgment about larger rhetorical issues. Two means of making such judgments, general impression and analytic scale evaluation procedures, have been widely used for several years. Since they have been described in detail by Conlon (1976), Cooper (1975), and Diederich (1974), I review these procedures only briefly. A relatively new evaluation procedure, primary trait scoring, requires a fuller discussion.

In doing an analytic scale or general impression evaluation, we assume that all writing in a given mode must have the same qualities. Consequently, we would read all expository writing with such questions as these in mind: Is the writing clearly organized? Are the ideas well-developed? Is the wording effective? Does the writer have a reasonable command of standard written English? An analytic scale asks readers to consider each of these matters separately, perhaps using a scale such as the following (Diederich, 1974):

	Low		Middle		High
General Merit					
Ideas	2	4	6	8	10
Organization	2	4	6	8	10
Wording	1	2	3	4	5
Flavor	1	2	3	4	5
Mechanics					
Usage	1	2	3	4	5
Punctuation	1	2	3	4	5
Spelling	1	2	3	4	5
Handwriting	1	2	3	4	5

By contrast with analytic scales, the general impression procedure does not require readers to make separate judgments about organization, wording, and the others. Instead, readers are asked to familiarize themselves with "range finders," sets of essays that illustrate different levels of performance on a given task. The number of levels may vary; for one assessment, ETS raters use four levels, for another, eight. But in any case readers would be shown a set of papers that reflect the very best performance on the assigned task, another set of papers that are somewhat less successful, and so on, with sets of range finders for each level.

In contrast with analytic scale and general impression procedures, primary trait scoring[13] rests on the assumption that different tasks, even different expository tasks, may have to be judged by different criteria. Qualities that are important for one sort of writing assignment may be irrelevant to or inappropriate for other kinds of tasks. Thus we would read different types of writing with different questions in mind. For example: one of the writing tasks for the 1974 National Assessment of Educational Progress-Writing (NAEP-W) asked students to write a letter in which they would try to persuade their principal that the school should be changed in some way and that the proposed change would be both practical and beneficial to the school. Another NAEP-W task asked students to express their opinion on this assertion: "A woman's place is in the home." As I noted above, readers of the "woman's place" essays were asked to consider two basic questions:

> Does the writer support his or her claims with elaborated reasons?
> Does the writer cite a variety of sources (personal experience, authority, books) in support of his or her reasons?

In reading the letters to the principal, judges were asked to consider a different set of questions:

> Does the writer identify a single problem that needed to be solved?
> Does the writer propose a solution?
> Does the writer show that the proposed solution is workable and beneficial?

For other assignments, the questions (and the criteria they imply) would vary.

In setting up criteria for a particular writing assignment, we would need to follow the basic procedure used in creating primary trait scoring guides for NAEP-W. That is, we would first need to analyze the assignment, asking such questions as these: Who is the audience? What characteristics are likely to be true of that audience? In the light of those audience characteristics, what rhetorical strategies are most likely to help accomplish the assigned purpose? After considering these questions, we would also need to analyze an extensive sample of student responses to the assignment. What strategies do students actually use in trying to do the assigned task? If, for example, the task is persuasive, have they used types of arguments that we did not anticipate in analyzing the assignment? From the analysis of both the assignment and student writing, we would formulate a list of qualities that seem important for writing a successful response to the assigned task. We would then train readers to look for these qualities as they evaluate student papers.

As will be evident in the following pages, I think primary trait scoring is quite useful. But when we decide to accept any scoring procedure, we must be very conscious of its assumptions and limitations (see Gere, 1980; Odell and Cooper, 1980). As Anne Gere has pointed out, primary trait scoring does not lead evaluators to consider such textual matters as cohesion. Thus it seems likely that evaluators may want to follow the practice of NAEP (1980) and supplement primary trait evaluation with analyses of errors, syntax, or coherence.

Another distinctive and potentially troublesome feature of primary trait scoring is that it restricts the issues judges are to consider as they evaluate student writing. This raises the possibility that, as Gere points out, judges will discount "writing which ventures outside the parameters of the given task or takes an unusual perspective on the issues involved." We may reduce the chances of penalizing students who take an unusual perspective if our primary traits are informed by our analysis of a large sample of student writing for a given task. We might also want to allow judges to submit to an evaluation leader those essays which appear to fulfill the assignment but do not display the characteristics we have asked judges to look for.

A piece of writing that "ventures outside the parameters of the given task" raises a more profound problem. Some evaluators assume that students should have great latitude in determining the form, purpose, and audience of their writing. Primary trait scoring, on the other hand, involves the assumption that writers must accept some constraints over which they have relatively little control.[14] For example: In this article I make some recommendations about evaluating writing. In making these recommendations, I anticipate that readers will raise several kinds of questions. What basis is there for recommending procedure X rather than procedure Y? How does procedure X compare with procedure Y? How can I actually carry out procedure X? The anticipation of these questions creates certain parameters within which I must work. Granted, I might have decided not to accept these parameters. But no matter what I decide, these questions will almost certainly arise. They constitute a constraint that is not entirely of my own creation.

My experience in writing and in working with writers in business and government (Odell and Goswami, 1980) leads me to conclude that writers may often have to accept such constraints. From the standpoint of primary trait scoring, it seems reasonable to assume that this conclusion pertains to student writers as well as to adults. Of course, if we accept this conclusion, we also accept the responsibility of continually reassessing our writing assignments and the criteria by which we judge student writing. Each time we assess student writing, we must determine whether our assignment and criteria are reasonable for a given group of students.

Any of the three preceding evaluation procedures can let us make reliable judgments about the relative quality of student essays. Any of the three can let us decide which essays are best, which are slightly less good, which are not acceptable at all. In practice, it seems a good idea to combine one aspect of ETS general impression scoring with either an analytical scale or primary trait scoring. Assume, for example, that we have decided to use a primary trait scoring guide that rates papers at one of four levels, ranging from *excellent* to *not competent*. (The exact number of levels may vary; as mentioned previously, ETS may use as few as four levels or as many as eight.) To make sure judges understood what we meant by an excellent paper, we would need to follow the ETS procedure of providing judges with "range finders" to illustrate the criteria we establish for assigning papers to a given level.

Many analytic scales address the issue of mechanics directly. That is, they ask readers to say whether a writer's command of certain aspects of mechanics (usage, spelling, punctuation, handwriting) is "low," "middle," or "high." General impression scoring does not ask readers to give a specific score or ranking to a student's use of mechanics. But papers selected as range finders often make it clear that mastery of mechanics is one of the bases for assigning papers to a certain level. By contrast with analytic scales and general impression procedures, primary trait scoring does not ask readers to consider mechanics. Since students' mastery of mechanics is important, we would have to supplement a primary trait scoring with an "error count" of the sort I have described above.

Combining Diagnosis and Evaluation

We can make reliable judgments about the quality of students' writing by using analytic scale, general impression, or primary trait scoring procedures. But of these procedures, primary trait scoring seems especially useful for combining diagnosis and evaluation. This combination is very important if we want the evaluation of writing to help with the task of teaching writing. That is, rank-ordering essays is not enough if we want our evaluation to help us see where students are having difficulty with writing or if we want to identify areas in which a school's writing curriculum might be changed.

To see how we might combine diagnosis and evaluation, consider scoring procedures devised for the NAEP-W "woman's place" writing task. These procedures first asked readers to use numbers 0–4 to indicate the number of reasons students gave to support their views and the extent to which students elaborated on their reasons.

0 = No response; fragment

1 = Does not take a clear position, or takes a position but gives no reasons
Position given, then abandoned
Position confused, or not defined at all
Position given, no reasons for it
Note: Taking a "middle of the road" position is acceptable

Example:

I think that a woman's place is in the home. I don't think that women should have to work. Its OK I wouldn't mind it. If a women wants to work which some do. That's fine. But if you have children I think you should stay at home with them. If its necessary to work then I guess that you have to work.

2 = Takes a position and gives one unelaborated reason

Example:

> I do not believe that a woman's place is in the home. Women
> shouldn't have to stay home all day cooking and cleaning,
> just because they're women. All human beings should be
> treated equal and this includes a well-educated woman
> being able to work at a job, instead of doing menial house-
> work tasks all day.

3 = Takes a position and gives one elaborated reason, one elaborated plus one unelaborated reason, or two or three unelaborated reasons

Example:

> I believe that a woman's place is at home because it would
> be easier on her to stay home and clean house, cook the
> meals and take care of the children if any. A working
> woman is usely easiler to be tired or ran down and taking
> care of the home too. She might not even have time for
> husband or children maybe even her home by trying to hold
> down a job. She wouldn't have time to take care of herself
> as she normally would or to have kids.

4 = Takes a position and gives two or more elaborated reasons,
one elaborated plus two or more unelaborated reasons, or
four or more unelaborated reasons

Example:

> A woman's place is not in the home. Women are human
> beings, it is their God given right to pursue what ever career
> they desire. Life, liberty and the pursuit of happiness have
> been mentioned in the Declaration of Independence yet
> women have been denied their rights in this sexist society.
> Not everyone wants to do the same job or pursue the same
> goals, must women be limited to a narrowly defined sphere
> of activity? No, a resounding no! We are people, human
> beings with as complex mental, emotional, physical needs
> as men, a fact ignored. We are regarded as the second sex,
> the incomplete sex, satisfied and made whole only by a
> family. And it is this false assumption shared by many men
> and women too, fostered by the society we live in that has
> destroyed many lives because people were not allowed to
> express the full range of their God given gifts and creativity.
> This attitude has been, is reinforced at every turn and what
> seem to be the most trivial points are often the most telling
> because they "go without saying." A fine example would
> be that in filling out the front cover, we are identified as
> female by number 2. These slights are equivalent to the
> demigration of Blacks in Westerns where the villains always
> wear black hats.

After determining how many elaborated and unelaborated
reasons a writer had given, judges were asked to indicate whether
students' essays contained one or more of the following appeals:

Conventional Wisdom: "I think this is just because the husband has always been known as the breadwinner."

Personal Experience: "I'm not used to having my mom at home all the time."

Authority: "Many famous American authors have said that women can take life better than men."

Analogy or Figurative Language: "Russia is a good example of equality for women, more women are doctors and women work in steel factories and do manual labor."

History: "Suppose great women like Mary McLeod Bethune had stayed in the home."

Legal Rights: "They have a right just as men do to go out and work."

Finally, readers were asked to indicate whether writers

1. Advanced appeals in support of their own position
2. Advanced appeals to refute opposing positions
3. Used appeals both to support their own view and refute opposing views
4. Made no use of the appeals mentioned above

Given the NAEP-W scoring procedures, we may speculate about criteria for judging students' responses to the assignment. We must remember, however, that the following sets of criteria can only be considered illustrative. In order for us to set up valid, useful criteria, the assignment should have specified the audience students were addressing, and we should have read a number of student responses to the assignment to make sure our criteria were actually appropriate.

In creating these sets of criteria, I have assumed that success with the given assignment requires students to make full use of the categories identified by NAEP-W. It is quite possible that for other writing tasks we would use somewhat different criteria. For example:

In "highly satisfactory" papers, the writer
1. Takes a position and gives two or more elaborated reasons, one elaborated reason plus two or more unelaborated reasons, or four or more unelaborated reasons
2. Uses three or more kinds of appeals
3. Uses these appeals both to advance the writer's own position and to refute opponent's position

In "satisfactory" papers, the writer
1. Takes a position and gives one elaborated reason, one unelaborated reason or two or three unelaborated reasons
2. Uses only two kinds of appeals
3. Uses these appeals either to advance the writer's own views or to refute opponent's views

In "minimally acceptable" papers, the writer

1. Takes a position and gives only two unelaborated reasons
2. Uses only one type of appeal

In "unacceptable" papers, the writer

1. Takes a position and gives only one unelaborated reason, takes no clear position, takes a position but gives contradictory reasons

We may, of course, make our criteria as stringent as seems reasonable, given our assignment and the general performance of our students. Had the "woman's place" assignment specified an audience, our criteria could probably have included some reference to aptness of diction and syntax and plausibility of reasons given. The important thing is that the sort of procedure I have described will do more than tell us which students are not performing acceptably on a given kind of task. It will help us see what problem(s) the student is having and will also help us determine what the student might do in order to improve on subsequent comparable tasks.

Three Types of Assessment

Simply as a part of our teaching, most of us are concerned with one basic question: Are individual students in our classes becoming more competent as writers? With the increasing public interest in accountability, teachers and evaluation specialists are also becoming concerned with two additional questions: Is our school's (or our school district's) writing program helping most of our students become more competent writers? Which students have not achieved at least minimum competence in their writing? To answer any of these questions, we need to follow the basic procedures described in the preceding section of this chapter. Other procedures may vary according to the type of question we want to answer.

Are Individual Students Improving as Writers?

To answer this question, we would need to keep a writing folder for each student; into this folder would go every piece of writing the student did during the year. Periodically we would look at selected pieces in the folder, judge them by criteria that had been discussed in class, and tell the student whether he or she was improving. This evaluation would serve as a diagnosis that let both teacher and student know what the student needed to do to improve. To obtain a more rigorous assessment of an individual student's growth for the year, we might proceed as follows:

1. Choose two pieces of writing done early in the year and two pieces of writing done late in the year (*Note:* All four of these must be comparable in audience and purpose; we would need to choose, for example, four pieces of persuasive writing intended for a general audience.)
2. Put the essays in two pairs, one early essay and one late essay in each pair
3. Remove student names and anything that would indicate when the essays were written
4. Give the pairs of papers to two readers who have been trained to judge papers according to criteria we have specified
5. For each pair ask the judges to specify which paper is the better

Is Our Language Program Helping Large Groups of Students?

This sort of assessment might involve students in a given grade, in a given junior high or senior high school, or in an entire school district. To answer our basic question (Considered as a group, are our students benefiting from our instructional procedures and materials?), we would proceed as follows. First, we would need to determine what kinds of writing we wanted to stress during the school year. For example, we might decide we wanted students to (1) write explanations that would be clear and helpful to an audience that had no direct knowledge of the subject; (2) express their feelings/ideas/perceptions to an interested, sympathetic audience. Then we would need to create four writing assignments, two for each of the two kinds of writing we were interested in. Each assignment would specify topic, audience, and purpose.

Early in the school year (within the first month), we would need to ask students to do two of these assignments—one of the explanatory assignments and one of the expressive assignments—as pretests. We would need to follow procedures described by Sanders and Littlefield (1975) and allow two class periods for each assignment, one period to write an initial draft and one period to revise and edit. For students who did not need the full second period, we could schedule an individualized activity such as sustained silent reading.

After collecting these pretest essays, we and our colleagues would need to meet, discuss the demands of the assignment, read some of the students' essays, and agree upon the primary traits that seemed essential for success with each kind of assignment. In subsequent writing assignments, we would stress these traits, using them as a basis for evaluation.

Near the end of the year—in April or May, some time before classtime is too disrupted by end-of-year activites—we would need to give two of the four writing assignments as posttests. Just in case these assignments might vary in difficulty, it would be a good idea to divide the total group of students into halves. Also, it would be useful to arrange the assignments thus: (1) explanatory assignment A; (2) expressive assignment A; (3) expressive assignment B; (4) explanatory assignment B. For their pretest, one half of the students would do assignments 1 and 3; the other half would do assignments 2 and 4. For the posttest, students who did assignments 1 and 3 as pretests would do assignments 2 and 4. Students who did assignments 2 and 4 as pretests would do assignments 1 and 3 as posttests. For each of the students, we would make two sets of writings, the pre and posttest explanatory pieces and the pre and posttest expressive writings. Before evaluating these papers, we would need to cover up or remove any information that would tell which student wrote the essays or when an essay was written.

With this preparation completed, the actual evaluation becomes relatively simple. Each essay would have to be read by at least two judges, who would use a list of primary traits to rank order the essays.

Assessing Minimum Competence

Of the three types of assessment mentioned in this chapter, minimum competence assessment is correctly receiving the greatest amount of attention. This attention is justified. All of us—teachers, parents, students, and the general public—deserve to know whether students can write with reasonable skill. But all of us should resist the tendency to equate minimum competence with mastery of the "rules" (spelling, punctuation) of writing. Important as this mastery is, we cannot assume that the ability to avoid serious mechanical errors implies even minimal skill in communicating effectively. Consequently, tests of minimum competence must be based on the same principles that govern all other efforts to assess students' writing performance.

In some states such as New York, the assessment of minimum competence may be carried out by a central agency such as a State Department of Education. In other states, such as Oregon, assessment of minimum competence is left up to individual school districts. If the evaluation is done by a central agency, teachers and administrators must do everything they can to make sure that the evaluation procedures do, in fact, measure writing ability and not just the ability to observe conventions of spelling and punctuation.[15] If the assessment is left to individual schools or school districts, minimum competency assessment should be a part of the regular program for assessing the writing ability of *all* students. Underlying this recommendation are several assumptions: that students of all ability levels can benefit from instruction in writing; that effective writing instruction depends on teachers' having a clear understanding of students' strengths and weaknesses as writers; that an evaluation which identifies only the poorest writers leaves us with the unnecessary burden of conducting yet another evaluation to identify the strengths and weaknesses of more able writers. The work of minimally competent writers will inevitably have some problems; when we look at their writing, we will find places where we can correct spelling or usage, think of more appropriate language, find more persuasive agreements. The question is: What kinds of problems are to be tolerated? Or, more positively: What strengths must be apparent in a piece of writing before we are willing to say that a particular student writes with a minimally acceptable level of skill?

To the best of my knowledge, we have no ready-made answers to these questions; there is no existing set of criteria that would let us make satisfactory, reliable decisions as to what would be minimally acceptable for students in every school district or state in the nation. Lacking such criteria, we will need to proceed as we would in doing any rank ordering of student writing. That is, we would need to decide upon appropriate criteria and illustrate those criteria with specific pieces of student writing. In following such a procedure, it seems very likely that the definition of "minimum competency" may vary from school district to school district or from state to state. For those who advocate some national standard of minimum competence, this variation will seem troublesome. But it may have the advantage of reflecting the specific strengths and weaknesses of students in a given area and of representing the values of citizens and teachers in that area.

A Final Note to Teachers and Researchers

The current interest in testing "competence" and "minimum competence" has brought protests from many members of our profession—understandably so, since this testing often involves evaluation procedures that are ill-conceived and misleading. One response to the testing movement is to point out fallacies in procedures used in assessing students' writing. But no matter how perceptive or reasonable we are in criticizing existing assessment procedures, criticism is not enough. The surest way to get rid of invalid assessment procedures is to replace them with something better. We must demonstrate that we have alternative procedures for assessment, procedures that will let us describe students' performance accurately and that will help us see what students need to do in order to write more competently on future assignments. State legislators and the taxpayers who support our schools have a right to expect us to provide such assessment. And so do our students.

Notes

1. "Minimal competence" is one of the most widely-used phrases in the current competency movement. I shall discuss assessment of minimum competence, but that discussion presumes some understanding of basic principles for assessing writing ability at all levels of competence.

2. Taken from the "Cross-sectional Sample of Writing Performance." Planned as a data-base for descriptive studies of writing performance, the design for the sample and the specific writing tasks were developed in early 1976 by Charles Cooper, Lee Odell, and Cynthia Watson. During the 1976-77 school year Charles Cooper and Cynthia Watson coordinated the gathering of the sample from school districts in New York, Michigan, and Illinois. Subsequently, Charles Cooper and Lee Odell supervised the primary-trait scoring of the sample.

3. Sanders and Littlefield (1975) report that community college students benefited from being able to choose their own topic (Sanders and Littlefield specified the students' purpose and audience.) and do some research prior to writing a first draft. The research was done outside of class; first drafts and revisions were done during two class periods. To guard against plagiarism, Sanders and Littlefield required students to turn in all notes and bibliographic references.

4. Rita Giglia, Tonawanda Junior High School, Tonawanda, New York

5. Donald McAndrew, Bishop Timon High School, Buffalo, New York

6. For a more detailed discussion of these and other questions, see Fred R. Pfister and Joanne F. Petrick's article, "A Heuristic Model for Creating a Writer's Audience" (1980). Also see James Moffett's *Teaching the Universe of Discourse* (1968) and James Britton's *The Development of Writing Abilities (11-18)* (1975).

7. This and the following tasks are selected from the "Cross-sectional Sample of Student Writing." See note 2, above.

8. This suggestion is contrary to the practice of many teachers who mark every error of every type. But as we categorize errors, we can focus the attempts of evaluators and thereby improve the reliability of their judgments. We can also increase our chances of understanding the strategies or processes which, according to Mina Shaughnessy (1977) and Barry Kroll and J. C. Schafer (1978), may be leading students to repeat a particular type of error.

9. Researchers may be interested in the much more detailed analytic scheme that appears in Mullis and Mellon (1980), pages 9-22.

10. Materials from the 1980 National Assessment point out that the presence of cohesive ties does not necessarily mean that an entire piece of writing will be coherent. It is possible for sentences in a section of a paper to be linked to each other and yet have no clear relationship to sentences in another part of the paper.

11. For a more detailed discussion of these cohesive ties, see the National Assessment of Educational Progress report, *Writing Achievement, 1969-1970*, pages 73-75.

12. Materials from National Assessment (1980) indicate that this rubric may be subject to revision. However, it did allow judges to make highly reliable decisions, and it appears to be a relatively simple way to obtain information about a complex matter.

13. For further information about primary trait scoring, see Ina V. S. Mullis' (1980) essay "Using the Primary Trait System for Evaluating Writing" and the reports of the National Assessment of Educational Progress.

14. I accept the claim of Walter Ong (1975) and of Russell C. Long (1980) that writers must define the role they expect their readers to play. I assume, however, that there may be limitations as to the role a writer may ask a given reader to play.

15. For an example of a statewide assessment procedure that meets many of the criteria I have discussed in this chapter, see the *Manual for Teachers and Administrators* prepared for the New York State preliminary competence test in writing. This document is available from the English Education Bureau, State Education Department, Albany, New York 12234.

References

Beach, Richard. "Self-Evaluation Strategies of Extensive Revisers and Non-Revisers." *College Composition and Communication* 27 (May 1976): 160-164.

Beaven, Mary. "Individualized Goal Setting, Peer Evaluation, and Self Evaluation." In *Evaluating Writing: Describing, Measuring, Judging*, edited by C. R. Cooper and L. Odell. Urbana, Ill.: NCTE, 1977.

Braddock, Richard. "The Frequency and Placement of Topic Sentences in Expository Prose." *Research in the Teaching of English* 8 (Winter 1974): 287-302.

Breland, Hunter M., et al. *A Preliminary Study of the Test of Standard Written English*. Princeton, N.J.: Educational Testing Service, 1976.

Britton, J., *et al. The Development of Writing Abilities (11-18)*. London: Macmillan Education, 1975.

Christensen, Francis. *Notes Toward a New Rhetoric*. New York: Harper and Row, 1967.

Competency Tests and Graduation Requirements. Reston, Va.: National Association of Secondary School Principals, 1976.

Conlon, Gertrude. *How the Essay in the CEEB English Test Is Scored*. Princeton, N.J.: Educational Testing Service, 1976.

Cooper, Charles R. "Holistic Evaluation of Writing." In *Evaluating Writing: Describing, Measuring, Judging*, edited by C. R. Cooper and L. Odell. Urbana, Ill.: NCTE, 1977.

Cooper, Charles R. "Measuring Growth in Writing." *English Journal* 64 (March 1975): 111-120.

Crowhurst, Marion, and Piche, Eugene. "Audience and Mode Discourse Effects on Syntactic Complexity in Writing at Two Grade Levels." *Research in the Teaching of English* 13 (May 1979): 101-109.

Diederich, Paul. *Measuring Growth in English*. Urbana, Ill.: NCTE, 1974.

Educational Testing Service. *Sequential Tests of Educational Progress: Writing Forms 1A and 1B and Manual*. Princeton, N.J.: Educational Testing Service, 1957.

Elbow, Peter. *Writing without Teachers*. New York: Oxford University Press, 1973.

Flower, Linda. "Writer-Based Prose: A Cognitive Basis for Problems in Writing." *College English* 41 (September 1979): 19-37.

Freedman, S. W. "Why Do Teachers Give the Grades They Do?" *College Composition and Communication* 30 (May 1979): 161-164.

Gere, Anne R. "Written Composition: Toward a Theory of Evaluation." *College English* 42 (September 1980): 44-58.

Gibson, Walker. *Persona*. New York: Random House, 1969.

Graves, Donald. "An Examination of the Writing Processes of Seven Year Old Children." *Research in the Teaching of English* 9 (Winter 1975): 227-241.

Halladay, M. A., and Hassan, R. *Cohesion in English*. London: Longman, 1976.

Hirsch, E. D. *The Philosophy of Composition*. Chicago: University of Chicago Press, 1977.

Hunt, Kellogg. *Grammatical Structures Written at Three Grade Levels*. Champaign, Ill.: NCTE, 1965.

Hunt, Kellogg. "Early Blooming and Late Blooming Syntactic Structures." In *Evaluating Writing: Describing, Measuring, Judging*, edited by C. R. Cooper and L. Odell. Urbana, Ill.: NCTE, 1977.

Kincaid, Gerald L. "Some Factors Affecting Variations in the Quality of Students' Writing." Ed.D. dissertation, (Michigan State College) Michigan State University, 1953. University Microfilm N. 5922.

Kroll, B. M., and Schafer, J. C. "Error Analysis and the Teaching of Composition." *College Composition and Communication* 29 (October 1978): 242-248.

Lloyd-Jones, Richard. "Primary Trait Scoring of Writing." In *Evaluating Writing: Describing, Measuring, Judging*, edited by C. R. Cooper and L. Odell. Urbana, Ill.: NCTE, 1977.

Long, Russell C. "Writer-Audience Relationships: Analysis or Invention?" *College Composition and Communication* 31 (May 1980): 221-226.

Macrorie, Ken. *Telling Writing*. Rochelle Park, N.J.: Hayden Book, 1970.

Meade, Richard, and Ellis, W. Geiger. "Paragraph Development in the Modern Age." *English Journal* 59 (February 1970): 219-226.

Mellon, John. *Transformational Sentence-Combining.* NCTE Research Report No. 10. Champaign, Ill.: NCTE, 1969.

Moffett, James. *Teaching the Universe of Discourse.* Boston: Houghton Mifflin, 1968.

Mullis, I. V. S. "Using the Primary Trait System for Evaluating Writing." Report No. 10-W-51. Denver, Co.: National Assessment of Educational Progress, Education Commission of the States, 1980.

Mullis, I. V. S., and Mellon, John. "Guidelines for Three Ways of Evaluating Writing." Report No. 10-W-50. Denver, Co.: National Assessment of Educational Progress, Education Commission of the States, 1980.

Murray, Donald. "Teach the Motivating Force of Revision." *English Journal* 67 (October 1978): 56–60.

National Assessment of Educational Progress. *Explanatory and Persuasive Letter Writing.* Writing Report No. 01-W-03. Denver, Co.: National Assessment of Educational Progress, Education Commission of the States, 1977.

National Assessment of Educational Progress. *Expressive Writing.* Writing Report No. 05-W-02. Denver, Co.: National Assessment of Educational Progress, Education Commission of the States, 1976.

National Assessment of Educational Progress. *The Third Assessment of Writing: Released Exercise Set.* Report No. 10-W-25, 1978–79. Denver, Co.: National Assessment of Educational Progress, Education Commission of the States, 1980.

National Assessment of Educational Progress. *Writing Achievement, 1969–79: Results from the Third National Writing Assessment, Vol. I—17 Year Olds.* Report No. 10-W-01, 1969–70, 1973–74, and 1978–79 Assessments. Denver, Co.: National Assessment of Educational Progress, Education Commission of the States, 1980.

National Assessment of Educational Progress. *Writing Achievement, 1969–79: Results from the Third National Writing Assessment, Vol. II—13 Year Olds.* Report No. 10-W-02, 1969–70, 1973–74, and 1978–79 Assessments. Denver, Co.: National Assessment of Educational Progress, Education Commission of the States, 1980.

National Assessment of Educational Progress. *Writing Achievement, 1969–79: Results from the Third National Writing Assessment, Vol. III—9 Year Olds.* Report No. 10-W-03, 1969–70, 1973–74, 1978–79 Assessments. Denver, Co.: National Assessment of Educational Progress, Education Commission of the States, 1980.

Odell, Lee, and Cohick, Joanne. "Writing about Literature . . ." In *On Righting Writing*, edited by O. Clapp. Urbana, Ill.: NCTE, 1975.

Odell, Lee, and Cooper, Charles R. "Procedures for Evaluating Writing: Assumptions and Needed Research." *College English* 42 (September 1980): 35–43.

Odell, Lee, and Goswami, Dixie. "Writing in a Non-Academic Setting." Xerographic Copy. State University of New York at Albany, Albany, New York, 1980.

Ong, Walter J. "The Writer's Audience Is Always a Fiction." *PMLA* (1975): 9–21.

Pfister, F. R., and Petrick, J. F. "A Heuristic Model for Creating a Writer's Audience." *College Composition and Communication* 31 (May 1980): 213–220.

Raygor, A. *Writing Tests, Forms A and B and Examiner's Manual* (McGraw-Hill Basic Skills System). Monterey, Calif.: CTB/McGraw-Hill, 1970.

Sanders, Sara E., and Littlefield, John. "Perhaps Test Essays Can Reflect Significant Improvement in Freshman Composition: Report of a Successful Attempt." *Research in the Teaching of English* 9 (Fall 1975): 145–153.

Shaughnessy, Mina. *Errors and Expectations.* New York: Oxford University Press, 1977.

Warriner, John, and Griffith, Frances. *English Grammar and Composition.* New York: Harcourt Brace and World, 1957.

Watson, Cynthia. "The Effects of Maturity and Discourse Type on the Written Syntax of Superior High School Seniors and Upper-Level College English Majors." Ph.D. dissertation, State University of New York at Buffalo, 1979.

Winterowd, W. Ross. "The Grammar of Coherence." In *Contemporary Rhetoric: A Conceptual Background with Readings,* edited by W. Ross Winterowd. New York: Harcourt Brace Jovanovich, 1975.

5 What It Means to Be Media Competent

Herb Karl
University of South Florida

This chapter is something of an anomaly in this book. It begins by arguing for the inclusion of its subject in school programs. No one doubts that language, reading, and writing are central to school programs or that they are the proper business of English language arts teachers; but most people, teachers included, have strong reservations about media studies in school programs. Or it may be that teachers and administrators simply don't see how to find space for media studies in already crowded curricula. At any rate, such studies have a limited place, if they appear at all.

My argument, developed and documented at length, is this: Since the electronic media in all their variety represent the dominant mass public communication mode, they deserve serious study in schools. Furthermore, in the context of this book, I am arguing that any serious approach to *assessment* of basic communicative competence in American schools in the years ahead must be concerned with media competence. I am making the assumption that the place for such studies and their assessment is in English programs. My view is that they deserve their own place, as in the new college and university departments of media studies and communications. But so far, where they have appeared in the schools, they have found a comfortable home among English teachers.

This chapter is also an anomaly in that there is no history of assessment (of measurement and evaluation) to point to in media studies. There are decades of psychometric work on language and reading, and recently there has been a surge of new developments in evaluation of writing. But so far in media studies everyone's efforts have been devoted primarily to theory, program development, and teaching methods. While this lack of assessment history made my task more difficult in one way, in yet another way it left me free with the challenge of conjecturing very tentatively about appropriate ways to assess media competence. I stop far short of specifying tests of *minimal* media competence, but so far as I know no state legislature is interested in that anyway.

My approach in this chapter is to extend gradually my description of media competence to include the following nonprint media: television, movies, radio, and recordings. As I discuss competence in viewing and/or responding to these media, I suggest a few ways teachers might assess a student's competence.

The Meaning and Purpose of Media Competence

Time use studies and consumer surveys (particularly those of A. C. Nielson and Elmo Roper) continue to unearth all manner of findings regarding the media habits of children and adults. Among other things, it appears that junior and senior high school students spend more time with electronic media (TV, records, radio, and movies) than they do with books; the average sixteen year old has spent as much time watching TV as attending school; many people find television a more believeable source of information than the daily newspaper; and finally, more American homes have TV sets than have indoor plumbing.

Such claims notwithstanding, several related questions on which there is little if any agreement continue to receive a considerable amount of attention from groups as diverse as the national PTA and congressional investigating committees. The questions have fueled the debate among educators on whether or not media studies should occupy the precious time of young people in school.[1] They include the following: Is TV or movie violence harmless? Is mass media advertising harmless? Does TV programming distort our perceptions of reality? Does TV news programming, in particular, tend to shape the events which are being reported? Does contemporary recorded music exert significant political and social influences on its listeners?

If you happen to believe the claims are generally true, and, furthermore, if you feel the questions are worth examining in school, you probably already possess a commitment to media competence, a concept which will be defined and occasionally redefined throughout this chapter.

The failure of school systems to make a commitment to media competence and the failure of teachers to involve students in the critical examination of the newer electronic communications media is seen by some as an ironic refusal to recognize a traditional educational responsibility—a responsibility not unlike that which led originally to the teaching of reading: namely, to prepare the young to cope with the dominant media of communication in their society. By abandoning that responsibility, the schools have implicated us all in a hazardous gamble with the future. At stake are not just the skills, but maybe the lives, of a generation of children. (Postman and Weingartner, 1974, p. 88)

The assumption underlying this quotation is of course that the electronic media have displaced print media as the dominant forms of mass communication.

The implications of such an assumption for the teacher of English have been the subject of a number of studies, most of which began appearing in the 1960s. Neil Postman's *Television and the Teaching of English* (1961) and Edmund J. Farrell's *English, Education and the Electronic Revolution* (1967) represented serious attempts to state the case for media study in English classrooms. In an article which appeared in *English Journal* 58 (November 1969), Bryant Fillion argued persuasively for the structuring of English around the three "cys": literacy, oracy, and mediacy. In adding mediacy to the traditional categories of literacy and oracy, Fillion raised these questions:

How do we educate our students to cope with mind- and behavior-shaping influences of the electronic media? How can our curriculum be adequate or relevant when the most powerful forces of communication in the world today are considered, if at all, as peripheral concerns of teachers? (p. 1232)

In these earlier studies a great deal of attention was given to the verbal message—the content or *what* is being communicated. Recently, emphasis has shifted to the medium itself—*how* a message is being communicated. The importance of the medium, the impact which medium has on meaning, underlies Marshall McLuhan's procrustean assertion: The medium is the message. What McLuhan is implying by this statement is that the medium (TV, radio, film) through which content is transmitted has as powerful an effect on an audience as content. In fact, some would claim that it is sometimes impossible to determine what is actually affecting an audience more—medium or message. Tony Schwartz in his book *The Responsive Chord* (1974) states unequivocally that no one understands precisely how the electronic media affect people:

Electronic media have been viewed merely as extensions of print, and therefore are subject to the same grammar and values as print communication. The patterned auditory and visual information on television and radio is not "content." Content is a print term, subject to the truth-falsity issue. Auditory and visual information on television or radio are stimuli that affect a viewer or listener.

> As stimuli, electronically mediated information cannot be analyzed
> in the same way as print "content." A whole new set of questions
> must be asked, and a new theory of communication must be for-
> mulated. (p. 19)

Even as concern mounts over the subtle effects which a particular medium may have on an audience, it is interesting to note a
corresponding concern over the issue of *who* has access to the mass
electronic media. Patrick Brantlinger (1978), for example, writes
that the problem of understanding the impact of TV is inextricably
bound up in

> the web of institutional controls and arrangements in which tele-
> vision is enmeshed in a given society. . . . Given its commercial
> base, American television is perhaps inevitably going to be low-
> brow rather than high-brow. But to reach that conclusion is also
> to suggest that the medium is not the message; it is only the chan-
> nel for messages otherwise determined. (pp. 89-90)

For Brantlinger and others like him, media competence is the
desired outcome of the careful study of the social, political, and
economic objectives of institutions which have access to communications media.

Regardless of the manner in which one chooses to develop media
competence—whether the focus of study is verbal content, the
medium itself, or the socio-political motives of powerful public
and private institutions—the question remains: What can English
teachers do to promote and evaluate media competence in their
students?

It would seem English teachers could provide students with the
skills to comprehend the verbal content of the various electronic
media—skills that John Mellon identifies as discourse, critical, and
appreciational. Moreover, attempts could be made to develop in
students the ability to determine the special effects of the medium
in which the content is "wrapped."

The verbal content skills associated with media competence
would probably not differ in kind from those expected from someone literate. The skills of interpretation and critical judgment are
as basic to media competence as they are basic to print literacy. A
media competent person, therefore, is one who at the very least is
able to

> distinguish between claims and appeals in advertising,
>
> recognize bias (social, economic, political, technical) in news

and entertainment programming, fictional or documentary films and broadcasts, and advertising,

distinguish between reports, inferences and judgments in news programming, and determine the effects of context on "the news."

While the special skills needed to cope with the nonverbal dimension of electronically mediated information remain controversial, if not illusive, enough is known about film and television to say that a competent viewer should be able to respond intelligently to the effects of shot composition, sound editing, motion, color, and lighting.[2] Such characteristics of form make it very obvious that electronically mediated communication requires more of a person than the ability to understand language. Essential differences exist between print and electronic media, and these differences must be taken into account in shaping a definition of media competence. For example, while print is arranged discursively (the eyes of the reader are greeted by symbols in linear and sequential order on the page), electronic media are nondiscursive (the eyes/ears of the viewer/listener are greeted by images on the screen/in the air for which patterns must often be created). Moreover, while print provides essentially "delayed" information (this morning's newspaper was printed last night), the electronic media have the potential to deliver immediate or "live" information. Additionally, certain electronic media provide great masses of people with simultaneous, though not necessarily "live," information which in turn generates effects that further differentiate these media. Ninety million people, for example, watched ABC's initial presentation of "Roots" on the same evenings at the same time in different places throughout America. Indeed, it is no wonder that the subjects of "Roots" found their way into countless English and social studies classes during the several days the production was aired. In sum, media competence would consist of the acquisition of content skills (which resemble higher order comprehension skills) and knowledge of the effects of the medium itself—those features principally visual and auditory which augment the senses and affect people in significantly different ways from print.

Only marginal efforts have been made in schools to develop media competence in students, and tests of media competence remain, for all practical purposes, nonexistent. Is this good or bad? Can such tests be developed? Ought they be developed? How do you really go about determining the ability of a person to interpret electronically mediated information?

Competence Is Complicated

One way we might begin to deal with such questions in this chapter is to simulate a process which a classroom teacher might go through in order to establish some estimation of the media competence of students. Let's say, for example, that a teacher wants to focus on TV advertising. This would seem to be reasonably justifiable in school curriculum if we did no more than randomly cite such information as the following: The average American at retirement age will have been exposed to more than fifty million advertisements, most of them on television. About twenty percent of all national television advertising is done by just three companies. Broadcast advertising rarely transmits a verifiable claim about the product, service, or idea being marketed. A prominent group of researchers (Liebert, Neale and Davidson, 1973) who studied the effects of television on young people has prompted them to conclude that "by age 11, children have become cynical about the purpose and credibility of commercials, feeling that they are being lied to in an attempt to get them to buy products which are not as desirable as the adman's copy would have it" (p. 131).

In any event, our hypothetical teacher desires to develop in students some basic TV advertising survival skills. First, an assumption is made about the language of advertising—namely, that it consists in part of statements which are verifiable, statements in other words that can be judged true or false. These true-false statements (or claims) are introduced and studied in class. As a test of competence in identifying verbal claims in TV advertising, students are asked by the teacher to view several commercials, making note of those statements which fit the definition of a claim. Thus, the process evolved in the classroom by the teacher yields a very specific media competency: *The student identifies advertising statements which are verifiable.* It should be pointed out that the strategy for determining the ability of students to demonstrate competence requires that they view actual TV commercials.

What makes the "claims" competency attractive to some is that it is very testable. For example, if a TV commercial states that a particular brand of wristwatch is waterproof, we know that a claim has been made, one that can be proven true or false under the appropriate conditions. To suggest, however, that such a competency yields even minimal understanding of the meanings and effects of TV advertising would be gross exaggeration. Though testable, it fails to reveal the spectrum of truth values that characterize advertising claims, since there are vague claims and irrelevant claims as well as precise claims and relevant claims. Moreover, the student's perception of TV advertising is restricted to verbal language. And, most importantly, we are not testing the critical judgment of students—the kind of judgment that responds to a question such as that which appears at the outset of this chapter: Is mass media advertising harmless? Genuine media competence permits a person to raise questions which in turn lead to judgments that show

what advertisements under what conditions are *harmful* to whom and for what reasons, or,

what advertisements under what conditions are *harmless* to whom and for what reasons, or,

what advertisements under what conditions are *helpful* to whom and for what reasons.

To avoid, in this process, dealing with the nonverbal aspects of TV advertising is to risk missing the whole point of what it means to be media competent. Though difficult to assess in an objective test—since so little is known about the possible effects generated by visual information and sound—some attempts have to be made to glean student responses to these vital meaning-making elements. The impact of sound in TV advertising, for example, is apparently capable of yielding such powerful effects on its audience that media critic Ron Rosenbaum (1975) finds himself both moved and puzzled by a new genre of commercials which he calls the inspirationals:

> You know the ones. Generally they have a large, vibrant chorus filling the background with a strong upbeat tune. Half hymn, half marching song, they are the national anthems of their products. On the screen crowds do energetic things such as jogging, marching and eating fried chicken while singing anthems, or getting ready to burst into song . . .
>
> [But] no matter how suspicious I get about them, the new inspirationals never fail to work their happy-making magic on me. That's what makes them so impressive, even scary. Inspirational technology has grown so sophisticated and powerful that TV commercial makers are capable of making one feel happy, *naturally* happy, without any sense of being manipulated into feeling happy. . . . (p. 55)

Though often not as subtle as auditory effects, the visual techniques of TV commercial-making can be just as surreptitious. The juxtaposition of visual images in order to shape the viewer's thoughts has been used since the beginning of TV advertising. For example, we are bombarded—in rapid alternation—with images of a popular soft drink and scenes of people surfing, skateboarding, playing games, etc., with the anticipated result that we associate the soft drink with moments of pleasure and excitement. We are being visually massaged into thinking that drinking a popular soft drink is inextricably linked with having a good time.

The point is simply this. Media competence implies much more than the identification of advertising claims. Understanding the meaning and effects of TV advertising requires a person to do more than decode the verbal messages of advertising. In addition to determining who is making the message, the intended audience, and what hidden assumptions underlie the message-making process, attention must be paid to the medium itself—the visual and/or auditory qualities which together with language contribute to the total meaning and effect of the advertising message.

In fact, if one were pressed to develop some items that would be used to assess the media competence of students in the area of TV advertising, it might not be unreasonable to expect some of the following:

> Select a TV commercial which makes no verbal claims. Since the ad does not resort to making a verbal claim explain how its selling message is communicated.
>
> Find a product advertised on TV which you judge to be non-essential and potentially harmful to you or other people. Explain the reasons for your judgment.
>
> Create a script for a TV commercial about a product, service or idea which you feel will be helpful to someone or some group. (The Sierra Club's "Activist Checklist," for example, contains a number of practical ideas for improving the environment.)

TV Drama and the Feature Film

As we shift attention from TV advertising to TV drama (which embraces all the various subgenre, including situation comedies) and the feature film, the need to develop in students the skill to deal with the visual and auditory elements of these media becomes increasingly apparent. Competence in responding to verbal content remains very important, but some proficiency is needed in what could be called the rhetoric of camera and sound.

When we ask students to demonstrate their competence in viewing films by asking them to respond to language or pictures and sound, we are actually asking them to recognize the tendency of the film's subject to be revealed to the viewer from a particular angle—whether the angle is that of a writer or that of a speaker or that of a camera. That is, we are asking students to recognize bias —social or technical. There are few more graphic examples of the need to develop a perspective on bias in film and televised drama than that illustrated by Leni Riefenstahl's *Triumph of the Will* which Joseph Goebbels released to the German public in 1937. While it was called a documentary, it remains in fact a cinematic fiction so subtle and powerful that it earned Miss Riefenstahl the right to be compared with Eisenstein as a master of film editing. An eminent critic of the period (Rother, 1960) wrote of the film:

> the deep feeling of uneasiness which *Triumph of the Will* arouses in unbiased minds originates in the fact that before our eyes palpable life becomes an apparition. . . . This film represents an inextricable mixture of a show simulating German reality and of a German reality maneuvered into a show. (p. 590)

The effect of this and similar films on the Nazi war effort was undoubtedly of considerable significance.

Neil Postman (1966) speaks directly to the matter of social bias in TV fiction when he states that the literature of television " may be used as a kind of index to the social values of the American community" (p. 187). Patrick Hazard (1966) in a publication of the National Council of Teachers of English writes that the "cultivation of judgment about TV programs and other manifestations of cultural democracy must surely be one of the primary responsibilities of the contemporary school" (p. 3). When you connect these remarks with those made about *Triumph of the Will*, it is possible to argue that the perception and understanding of bias is central to determining the meaning and effects of film and TV drama.

In a book designed especially for teachers of mass media, Robert Cirino (1977), a high school English teacher, has prepared what appears to be an excellent description of how a person attains competence in the viewing of film and TV drama. Anyone who can accept the exercise of critical judgment and the identification of bias as legitimate goals underlying the competent viewing of film and TV drama will find Cirino's book extremely useful. He stresses the importance of providing opportunities for students to watch a TV drama or feature film, to analyze it, to follow up with an evaluation of the impact on the audience, and to create alternative versions. If one were to use Cirino's ideas as a point of departure for developing a test of media competence, one might end up with items like these:

After viewing the drama, write a condensed version in which you provide samples of the original dialogue. Then answer the following questions:

What assumptions are made about criminals? For example, are you led to believe that organized crime can control the police?

What assumptions are made about the police? For example, are you led to believe that the public does not appreciate the police as much as it should?

What assumptions are made about the local, state, and national government? For example, are you led to believe that federal law enforcement officials don't cooperate as equals with local policemen?

Is there a prevailing political or social bias in evidence? For example, are the crimes which are committed distinctly blue collar crimes or crimes of the impoverished or socially ostracized?

Are there particular emotional appeals in evidence? For example, is a clear attempt made to create a contemptible villain whom you are made to feel deserves whatever he gets? Does the portrayal of violence serve a purpose or is it inserted of its own sake?

Write an alternative version of the film or TV drama you've just viewed in which you transform the main character into a totally different kind of person.

The substance of these items is designed to evoke the kinds of perceptions and thoughts about televised and filmed drama that will enable a student to make the judgments necessary to discover or uncover bias. In defense of such a goal, Donald Lazere (1977) has stated:

If English is to fulfill the Arnoldian ideal of seeing life steadily and whole, it must address itself to the primary social function of mass culture today, its all pervasive role in shaping political and social consciousness.

[The] most recent studies of the influence of television and other mass media on declining literacy rates have defined literacy narrowly in terms of fundamental reading and writing skills and have focused on TV only insofar as it is a visual rather than written medium. If literacy is defined, as it should be, in the larger sense of breadth of knowledge and capacity for reason, then it is evident that the greatest threats to literacy in the twentieth century are mass-mediated political thought control and the reason-numbing effects of mass culture, and that English, as the discipline preeminently responsible for fostering literacy, must provide critical weapons for combatting these anti-rational forces. (p. 754)

The arsenal of critical weapons for coping with film and TV consists, as has been suggested already, of more than questions about verbal content. The camera, for example, appears to have the capacity to generate a technical bias which can create meanings and effects distinct from, yet frequently complementing, the words that actors speak and the things that actors do. Possessing some minimal knowledge of what is meant by technical bias would seem to be a necessary adjunct to critical judgments about the verbal content of film and television.

Of all the technical aspects of film and television, shot composition is at once the most conspicuous and the most pervasive (see Figures 1–4). When a person views a movie and finds himself feeling some sense of morbid fascination during a scene of extreme violence, his competence in understanding the technical structuring of the scene will make the difference between being manipulated into feeling that violence is enjoyable or knowing that the director, cameraman, and film editor have collaborated to produce such an effect. Because it is photographed from multiple angles in slower than normal slow motion, the scene portraying the death of Bonnie and Clyde in the Arthur Penn film is transformed into what is now referred to with almost classical regard as a *danse macabre*. Thus, what we would expect to find repugnant is given aesthetic dimension by the structuring of space (through camera angle) and time (through the speed at which the shooting is done). The connotations of a shot in a sequence of shots can be as powerful as the connotations of a word in a sentence.

If we were to assess a person's knowledge of the features of shot composition elemental to understanding a rhetoric of the camera, we might want to know, among other things, the extent to which that person can recognize and explain the possible meanings and effects suggested by

the sense of distance perceived between viewer and subject

the angle at which the camera is placed with respect to the subject

lighting and color tones

camera speed at which a shot is recorded

transition techniques between shots

cropping (i.e., isolating the camera eye on a certain part of a larger scene)

Figure 1. Connotations of strength and dominance are suggested by manipulating the perceived distance between the viewer and the characters depicted in Shot 1 (top) and Shot 2 (bottom). Shot 1 is a relatively close shot, whereas Shot 2 is a relatively long shot.

Figure 2.   Connotations of strength and dominance are also suggested by manipulating the succession of angles at which the viewer is permitted to view the above sequence of shots. Shot 1 (top) is typically referred to as a low angle shot (the camera is aimed upward at the subject) as compared to the high angle shot (Shot 2, bottom) in which the camera is mounted above the subject and aimed downward.

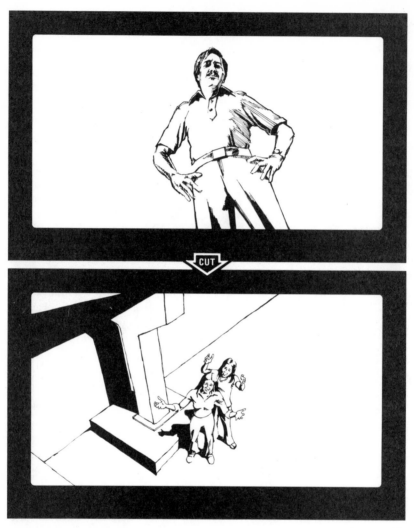

Figure 3. By manipulating both the perceived distance and the angle of perception (Shot 1, top, is a relatively close, low angle shot, while Shot 2, bottom, is a relatively long, high angle shot), the combined or synergetic effect becomes greater than the sum of the effects of each of the four (close, long, high, low) separate shots.

Figure 4. When the special visual techniques of the dramatic fictional film used, for example, in routine TV news reporting, the technical bias of shot composition merits serious attention in any attempt to judge the meanings and effects of such reporting on the viewer.

Becoming aware of the meaning and effects of visual devices such as these is one—but by no means the only—prerequisite to coping with the nonverbal elements of movies and television. What Ron Rosenbaum said about the impact of sound in TV commercials applies equally to TV drama and the feature film. The manner in which sound, or the lack of it, is used to manipulate audiences merits particular consideration in any efforts to evalute the competence of the film or television viewer.

Media competence in film and television has been narrowly construed here to mean the ability to discover or uncover bias in the verbal content and nonverbal structure of these media. So far in this chapter I have given no explicit attention to movies or TV programs as works of art. A well made film, to some, "has a power not yet equaled by that of any other medium to capture and satisfy the mass audience" (Sheridan, Owen, Macrorie, and Marcus, 1965, p. vii). However, to approach TV drama or the feature film as belles lettres—as art forms of the highest order—would be, for the most part, presumptuous. After all, most of the products have not been around long enough to have attained the permanence of a *Hamlet* or *Huckleberry Finn*. At the same time, it would be a serious mistake to assume that there is nothing to be gained from the careful analysis of the so-called film or TV classic. The value of such an activity is well documented. Besides it is difficult to take issue with the suggestions of Wilbur Schramm, Jack Lyle, and Edwin B. Parker (1961) who have prepared perhaps the most reputable sociological study of the effects of television on young people:

> Anything to which children devote one-sixth of their waking hours has obvious importance for schools. If children are helped to know good books from poor ones, good music from poor music, good art from bad art, there is no reason why they should not be helped to develop some standards for television. . . . It seems to us all to the good to bring television into the real-life process of learning, to break down the barrier between passive fantasy experience and active use. (pp. 184-185)

Nonetheless, we are not talking about TV or film appreciation in this chapter. We are talking about basic media competence—one's ability to identify and question the views of reality which are being communicated through film or television during a particular interval of time. This is not to suggest that studying film in the same manner one would study literature is of no value. In fact, the distinction between what has been talked about in this chapter as the discovery of bias (social and technical) and the study of film as art will be blurred to some readers. Much of what is to be found in *The Motion Picture and the Teaching of English* (Sheridan *et al.*, 1965) will be useful to someone struggling to determine what it means to be a competent viewer of movies. The same can be said of Howard Poteet's *The Compleat Guide to Film Study* (1972) and David Coynik's *Film: Real to Reel* (1972).

More adequate critical judgments about these media require that attention also be paid to questions such as the following: What is the effect of stereotyping (situations, characters, and values)? What do the "ratings," Emmy's, and Academy's mean? Does fictional violence cause real violence? To what extent are racism and sexism still a problem? What effect will recent Supreme Court rulings on obscenity and pornography have on the presentation of feature films?

So far, we've explored the concept of media competence with a focus on certain competencies needed to cope with the nonverbal form and verbal content of TV advertising, movies, and TV drama.

We've defined and redefined what it means to be competent in each medium—to be able to render critical judgments about the meanings and effects of a TV commercial, a film, or TV drama. We've even speculated on what test items of media competence might look like. We're ready now to take a fairly comprehensive look at another electronically mediated communication phenomenon—broadcast news and public affairs programming—and some of the basic knowledge and skills needed to cope with it.

News Programming

The power of news and public affairs programming is made rather explicit in an oft-quoted anecdote pertaining to the Kennedy-Nixon debates of the 1960 presidential campaign. After a viewing of one of the debate videotapes, John Kennedy is alleged to have turned to his press secretary, Pierre Salinger, and said: "We wouldn't have had a prayer without that gadget." JFK had just intuited the mystifying power of the medium of television as a transmitter of information about public affairs. Three years later, a poll conducted by Elmo Roper confirmed Kennedy's intuition. In 1963, Roper reported that television had not only replaced newspapers as the primary source of news for most people, but was regarded as the most "believable" of all the mass media. These curious facts coupled with Thomas Jefferson's conviction that the survival of the nation depended on an informed electorate provide some justivication for the need to understand what news is, how news is reported, what kinds of meanings are to be made of the news and news media, and what effects news and news media can have on the shaping of attitudes, beliefs, and actions.

The need to pay attention to such matters is even more apparent if we believe anthropologist Edmund Carpenter's (1977) assertion that televised newscasts and public affairs programs are being transformed into a new form of entertainment, one that offers

> cliché drama costumed as news. The commentator occupies the screen most of the time, though his visual appearance is totally irrelevant: Irrelevant to the news, but not irrelevant to the drama of the news hour, which is something utterly different, its own reality, with the commentator as star. (pp. 15-16)

The current practice on the part of the networks of raising newspeople to celebrity status, of paying large sums of money for what is often little more than reading the news in front of a TV camera, gives substance to Carpenter's assertion.

There is also the charge that the news media have begun to significantly influence the events which are supposed to be reported objectively—that important political events are scheduled to coincide with news media deadlines and that Spiro Agnew may have made a legitimate observation when he framed the following question: "How many marches and demonstrations would we have if the marchers did not know that the ever-faithful TV cameras would be there to record their antics for the next news show?"

Since television is far and away the most widely used source of information about the news and public affairs, it stands to reason that this communications medium ought to be given some attention in schools which lay claim to the goal of developing literate and responsible citizens in a democratic society.

First, though, it's important to understand that regardless of the medium, there are some essential awarenesses which every reader, listener, or viewer has to bring to a news report. Charles Weingartner (Postman, 1966) puts it this way:

> At the very least, we must be able to distinguish among factual, inferential, and judgmental statements. Unless one can recognize a fundamental difference between the statement, "Senator Mundt asked the witness twelve questions in half an hour," and the statement, "Senator Mundt harassed the witness," one is, of course, hopelessly unprepared to evaluate the news. (p. 113)

The distinction between reports, inferences, and judgments is not that much removed from the distinction made earlier between advertising claims and appeals. Like advertising claims, news reports are capable of being verified. And like advertising appeals, inferences and judgments have more to do with a person (in the case of the news, the reporter) than with the event being reported. Since reports, to some extent, are verifiable, any news story which does not subscribe to the language of reports is using the label "news" in a specious manner. Two obvious points need to be made here: (1) Any report is the result of any number of intervening judgments; (2) Such variables as voice intonation and camera angle can have the effect of transforming reports into judgments. This is not to say that inferences (statements about the unknown which are based on the known) and judgments (expressions of approval or disapproval) have no place in news programs. There is no question that the First Amendment to the Constitution gives the press the right to comment on as well as report the news. By making inferences and judgments about what it reports as news, a free press can challenge any belief, any law, any institution, any body that it feels needs to be challenged.

Responsible citizens, Jefferson would surely have argued, need to know when the press is reporting the news and when it is commenting on the news. Responsible citizens, in other words, need to be competent consumers of the news. Developing such competence and determining its attainment, therefore, can be looked upon as legitimate functions of the educational process. The problem of writing adequate test items for news comprehension competence is not much different from that of writing adequate test items for broadcast advertising, TV drama, and film. Here are some possible items:

> Read the fictional news article below. Assume that it is a transcript of a TV news segment:
>
>> MARS—The United Nations of Earth were embarrassed here yesterday for the first time in interplanetary sports history.
>>
>> The Earthling soccer team was hammered by the Martians 4-0 before 75,570 Martian citizens at Crater Stadium.
>>
>> "It's the worst game I've ever seen us play," said Earthling goalkeeper Melvin Birdsong. "Of course, the fact that the Martians have two extra legs didn't help us either," he added.
>>
>> If the Earthling team is to have a chance to win in the future, it appears that some system for handicapping Martian players will have to be devised by the Interplanetary Sports Council.
>
> Which of the statements in the story are reports?
>
> How would you go about verifying the reports?
>
> Which of the statements are inferential?
>
> Which of the statements are judgmental?
>
> If you were a news editor, would you accept the story as a news report? If not, how would you turn it into a news report?

There is at least one other item that should probably appear on a list of basic understandings about the language of news reporting. It has to do with the general semantic principle which states, in essence, that one cannot know the meaning of what one is perceiving unless something is known about the contexts or environments which affect perceptions. You can't know the meanings, in other words, unless you know the contexts. There are many contexts. The most obvious is the immediate verbal context. Taken out of its immediate verbal context, the following statement allows us to draw a number of inferences: "The Russians don't like to fight. They would rather attack us with finesse, which they will do if we give them the opportunity." The political and martial tones of the quote dissolve rather quickly once we are told that it came from the mouth of a Canadian ice hocky coach moments before a match with a Russian team. Getting at the effects of immediate verbal contexts can be illustrated for students with an activity like this:

Below are statements which cannot be understood adequately without knowledge of their immediate verbal contexts. Create an original context for each in order to clarify meaning.

Motorcycle racing is dull.

Too much skiing is likely to give you blisters.

Spaghetti will kill you.

The context principle actually takes us beyond the language content of news into the effects of the medium itself. Consider the effect that the limitations of air time imposes on broadcast news reporting. A story which can be reported in detail in a newspaper must be reduced considerably for use on a typical news broadcast. To get an idea of just how dramatic the change is, consider the following:

Select what you judge to be an important front page report from your local newspaper. Read the article aloud, noting exactly how long it takes to complete the reading. Now go back over the article deleting sentences in an attempt to reduce the reading time to thirty seconds. You have just approximated the task of a TV or radio news editor.

How much of the original meaning, if any, is lost in the version edited for TV?

Did you make any inferences in the edited version?

Imagine the job of the TV film editor who must take thirty minutes worth of film footage and reduce it to thirty seconds to accompany the verbal report. How different are the problems of the film editor from those of the news editor?

Our primary goals in assessing media competence in the area of broadcast news programming can be reduced to that of determining the ability of a person to distinguish among reports, inferences, and judgments, to estimate the effects of context (both verbal and technical) on perception of the news, and to recognize bias. An obvious debt is owed in this section to the principles of a brand of linguistic study commonly known as general semantics. In fact, much of this chapter—insofar as it addresses itself to matters of competence in understanding the verbal content of media—draws heavily on knowledge of a very practical nature to be found in S. I. Hayakawa's *Language in Thought and Action* (1972).

There are, of course, other important questions that must be asked in order to get a comprehensive sense of the meaning and effects of the form and content of broadcast news. These include: Can there really be objectivity in news reporting? Do all the networks report the same event in the same manner? How do news and editorial policies vary among the networks and local stations?

What is known about the censorship of specific news items and programs? What are the effects of private subsidization (advertising) on news and editorial policy? To what extent do the networks and local stations observe the Equal Time Provision and the Fairness Doctrine? To what extent are the news media being exploited by those who would attract news coverage in order to make money? The Committee on Public Doublespeak of the National Council of Teachers of English has been raising questions of this type for the past several years in an attempt to alert people to the necessity of examining the rhetoric of those who have access to the mass media.

The Electronic Enigma: Recorded Music

Some will argue that neither news programming, TV advertising, TV drama, nor the feature film has exerted as much social and political influence on America's youth as has the LP record and the local disc jockey. According to music critic Nik Cohn (Valdes and Crow, 1973), recorded music

> mirrors everything that happens to teenagers in this time, in this American twentieth century. It is about clothes and cars and dancing; it's about parents and high school and being tied and breaking loose; it's about sex and getting rich and getting old; it's about America. . . . (p. 235)

Any attempt, therefore, to define what it means to be media competent would be lacking something if it didn't attend to such questions as: Who listens to what on the radio? In what ways do recording artists appeal to their listeners? What attitudes and values do recording artists seem to promote in their music and lifestyles? Are auditory media (radio, records, tapes) more engaging sensory experiences than those of TV and the movies? How does the "character" of radio and recordings shape meaning and effects?

The questions to be raised and the items to be constructed around the lyrics of recorded music could follow a strategy not that much different from what has already been proposed by Robert Cirino for the analysis of TV drama. The outcome of such analysis ought to enable students to identify underlying social and political biases. But as many a teenager will quickly point out, such an activity is at the very least incomplete—since it ignores the beat, the melody, the whatever—and at the very most an invasion of privacy. For youth has perennially adopted current popular music as its personal property. To some teenagers, it's almost an encroachment on territorial rights for schoolteachers to give class time to studying the meanings and effects of what the DJs are playing and what the popular artists are saying.

Not only teenagers but grownups as well have questioned the value of looking for meaning and predicting effects of electronic media by focusing exclusively on verbal language. To Tony Schwartz (1974), a competent judge of the meaning and effects of recorded music knows something about how brain, sounds, and language merge into a state of emotional symbiosis. H. E. Krugman's (1970) studies indicate that the character of brain wave activity during exposure to television indicates that humans respond to TV and printed matter in significantly different ways. The more recent attempts to study brain functions (especially those attempts prompted by the work of neurosurgeons Roger Sperry and Joseph Bogen) promise to further illuminate the effects of media on human behavior. One thing is certain: We are in a tenuous area now, where media competence is as much a measure of feelings as it is a measure of rational intelligence.

The prospect of having to unravel the mysteries of how the brain makes meanings out of recorded music—or how it makes meaning out of the augmented sensory information of TV and the movies as well—is enough to blunt the enthusiasm of any testmaker. It would be ironic indeed if some time in the future we were to discover that Schwartz's hypothesis turns out to be the only basis for developing and testing media competence—that all the traditional concerns rooted in the verbal content of media are dwarfed by the effects which the medium itself has on the human brain. Such possibilities have the positive effect of making sure that any current attempts to assess media competence must be regarded as primitive and tentative.

Conclusion

The fact remains, however, that electronic media dominate a significant portion of the lives of children and adults. And for schools to ignore this fact—to abdicate responsibility for developing some degree of media competence is nothing less than, as Postman and Weingartner have already warned, "a hazardous gamble with the future."

It would seem that we are capable marginally of meeting the challenge. We can at least develop (and evaluate) some higher order literacy skills by providing students with opportunities to respond to the verbal content of electronically mediated information; and we can develop some lower level awareness of form by helping students understand the structural and technical features of electronically mediated information. We can also, whenever possible, engage students in certain media activities (filmmaking, video and audio taping, still photography), thus providing an experience-related awareness of the possible effects of the commercial uses of such media.

Undeniably, students must find ways to demonstrate informed and intelligent responses to the media which so dominate their lives. These responses need not take the form exclusively of tests of media competence. Writing a letter, conducting a counter-advertising campaign, making use of the radio and TV broadcast time guaranteed every citizen under the law—all of these options can be nurtured in schools. Students must be encouraged to act as well as think critically about the media. The willingness to speak up, to resist the temptation to passively accept, is probably the best indicator of media competence we shall ever devise.

Notes

1. The U.S. Office of Education has taken a firm stand on the need for media studies in the schools. In October, 1980, it unveiled its $1.6 million investment in the development of school programs in the critical viewing of TV. This effort is the first of its kind for the U.S. Office of Education and is supposed to yield programs and materials which will enable students at all levels (kindergarten through college) to analyze both their own TV viewing habits and the messages they receive from the medium. Classroom courses on critical viewing skills will be offered for four different grade levels and are being developed by four different groups: the Southwest Educational Development Laboratory (SEDL) in Austin, Texas (kindergarten through fifth grade); WNET/New York's education department (grades six through eight); the Far West Laboratory for Educational Research and Development in San Francisco (grades nine through twelve); and Boston University's School of Public Communications (post-secondary). The Far West Lab has subcontracted WGBH in Boston for a curriculum that may be used as a one semester elective or as part of an existing course. Debra Lieberman, project associate at the Far West Lab, states that the course will increase skills in the basics of reading, writing, critical thinking, research, debate, and math: "The list is endless when you realize that television is a communication medium with content that can be studied and approached in a wide variety of ways."

2. For an academic discussion of the structural devices of film, see Louis D. Giannetti's *Understanding Movies* (Englewood Cliffs, N.J.: Prentice-Hall, 1972). For a less academic approach to the same subject, see James Morrow and Murray Suid's *Moviemaking Illustrated: The Comic Filmbook* (Rochelle Park, N.J.: Hayden Book Company, 1973).

References

Brantlinger, P. "What Hath TV Wrought: McLuhan's 'global village' or Kosinski's 'village videot'?" *Media & Methods* 14 (April 1978): 36-41; 89-91.

Carpenter, E. *Oh, What a Blow That Phantom Gave Me!* Toronto: Bantam Books, 1972.

Cirino, R. *We're Being More Than Entertained.* Honolulu: Lighthouse Press, 1977.

Cirino, R. *Power to Persuade.* Toronto: Bantam Pathfinder Editions, 1967.

Comstock, G. *Television and Human Behavior: The Key Studies.* Rand, June, 1975.

Coynik, D. *Film: Real to Reel.* Winona, Minn.: St. Mary's College Press, 1972.

Farrell, E. J. *English, Education, and the Electronic Revolution.* Champaign, Ill.: NCTE, 1967.

Foster, H. M. *The New Literacy: The Language of Film and Television.* Champaign, Ill.: NCTE, 1976.

Giannetti, L. D. *Understanding Movies.* Englewood Cliffs, N. J.: Prentice-Hall, 1972.

Hayakawa, S. I. *Language in Thought and Action.* New York: Harcourt Brace Jovanovich, 1972.

Hazard, Patrick D. *TV as Art.* Champaign, Ill.: NCTE, 1966.

Innis, H. *The Bias of Communication.* Toronto: University of Toronto Press, 1951.

Johnson, N. "What Television Teaches." *The National Elementary Principal* 50 no. 5 (1971): 6-13.

Karl, H. "Media Literacy: The Right to Know." *English Journal* (October 1974): 7-9.

Karl, H. "Mass Con: In Search of Media Meanings." *Media & Methods* (May/June 1976): 32-33.

Krugman, H. E. "Brain Wave Measures of Media Involvement." *Journal of Advertising Research* 11 no. 1 (1971):3-9.

Krugman, H. E. "Passive Learning from Television." *Public Opinion Quarterly* 34 (1970): 184-190.

Kuhns, W. *Exploring Television.* Chicago: Loyola University Press, 1971.

Lazere, D. "Mass Culture, Political Consciousness and English Studies." *College English* 38 no. 8 (1977): 751-767.

Liebert, R. M.; Neale, J. M.; and Davidson, E. S. *The Early Widow: Effects of Television on Children and Youth.* New York: Pergamon Press, Inc., 1973.

Littell, J. F. *Coping with Television.* Evanston, Ill.: McDougal Littell, 1973.

McLaughlin, F. *The Mediate Teacher: Seminal Essays on Creative Teaching.* Philadelphia: North American Publishing Company, 1975.

McLuhan, M. *Understanding Media.* New York: New American Library, 1964.

Morrow, J., and Suid, M. *Moviemaking Illustrated: The Comic Filmbook.* Rochelle Park, N.J.: Hayden Book Company, 1973.

Postman, N. *Television and the Teaching of English*. New York: Appleton-Century-Crofts, 1961.

Postman, N. *Language and Reality*. New York: Holt, Rinehart and Winston, 1966.

Postman, N., and Weingartner, C. *The School Book*. New York: Delacorte Press, 1974.

Poteet, H. *The Compleat Guide to Film Study*. Champaign, Ill.: NCTE, 1972.

Rosenbaum, R. "Soap Gets in Your Eyes." *New Times*, 12 December 1975, pp. 51-56.

Rother, P. *The Film till Now*. New York: Twayne Publishers, 1960.

Schramm, W.; Lyle, J.; and Parker, E. B. *Television in the Lives of Our Children*. Stanford, Calif.: Stanford University Press, 1965.

Schrank, J. *Understanding Mass Media*. Skokie, Ill: National Textbook Center, 1975.

Schrank, J. *TV Action Book*. Evanston, Ill.: McDougal Littell, 1974.

Schwartz, T. *The Responsive Chord*. Garden City, N.Y.: Anchor Books, 1974.

Sheridan, M. C.; Owen, H. H., Jr.; Macrorie, K.; and Marcus, F., eds. *The Motion Picture and the Teaching of English*. New York: Appleton-Century-Crofts, 1965.

Sohn, D. *The Problem and the Promise: A Television/Video Workshop*. Pyramid Films, 1978.

Valdez, J., and Crow, J. *The Media Works*. Dayton, Ohio: Pflaum/Standard, 1973.

6 The Politics of
Minimum Competency

Miles Myers
University of California, Berkeley

Legislators who have authored and supported minimum competency legislation often view the minimum competency movement as an effort to restore the public's faith in and support of public education. Americans have had great faith in the public schools to solve social problems—redistribute wealth, eliminate racism, provide skilled labor for a technological-industrial society—but schools have often promised more than they could deliver, particularly when categorical aid became the vogue. Under categorical aid programs, every problem that came along, from drugs to delinquency, became a way for schools to get extra money if they proposed a solution. Much of the current pessimism about the schools results from too many promises which were not and could not be kept.

The pessimism also results from lack of knowledge about what schools have, in fact, accomplished. For example, Ralph Tyler, one of the founders of National Assessment of Educational Progress (NAEP), reports that the evidence from tests given draftees suggests that in World War I only about 45 percent of the seventeen year olds could read at a nine-year-old level. Now about 80 percent can (*Phi Delta Kappan*, March 1977). Furthermore, the schools are now attempting to educate students who formerly dropped out or were pushed out. In 1944, only 47 percent of California's eighteen year olds were in school. Now about 90 percent are.

Despite the great gains that schools have made in attempting a program of universal literacy, the current pessimism about the schools continues. One reason is that any gains in literacy are often offset by demands for higher levels of literacy to run our technical-industrial economy. Paper pushing jobs keep increasing while jobs for unskilled labor decrease. Some observers believe that the minimum competency movement will help schools meet technical-industrial demands by giving schools a proper goal setting procedure. In any case, the criticism of public institutions is to some degree a measure of the success of the schools. The more literate the population becomes, the more it will criticize public services.

Problems for Schools

Although the goal setting procedure of the minimum competency movement may improve the public's understanding of what schools do, the same procedure may have negative results if teachers are not sensitive to problems in three areas: how schools are financed, how students are tracked and distributed, and how curriculum decisions are made. First, how schools are financed.

Financial Pressures

In a political atmosphere requiring reduced public expenditures in all areas, professional statements of minimum competencies can be used as a rationale for cutting costs. Everything *beyond* the minimum becomes by definition a frill which public funds are not obligated to support. Reading programs, for example, are funded by Title I and Right to Read as a part of the public commitment to basic literacy for all citizens. Literature programs are not. Literature programs must turn for special funding to such agencies as the National Endowment for the Humanities, which has comparatively few public school projects.

How then, can literature programs be justified as part of a school program for teaching the minimum competencies? Political realities suggest that the appreciation of literature must be justified as part of the basic reading program. It seems self-defeating to organize the teaching of literature and the teaching of reading as entirely different activities.

The separation of reading and literature is consistent with sensitivities within the profession—the insistence of some literature teachers that they are *not* reading teachers, the fear of some English scholars that association with reading will undermine their professional credibility—but the separation is indifferent to the political realities which govern schools. If literature is not defined as a necessary part of the reading program, then it is literature which will be dropped if minimum competencies are used to rationalize reductions in funds for public schools.

How can one justify an appreciation of literature as one of the minimum competencies for reading? R. P. Blackmur ("Toward a Modus Vivendi," *The Lion and the Honeycomb*, New York: Harcourt, Brace and World, 1954) over twenty-five years ago warned that universal education was producing a new illiteracy, people who can read the words but not interpret, who can know literal meanings but not the purposes of the writer. Such people, said Blackmur, can be controlled and manipulated by demagogues using posters, flyers, newspapers. In fact, such people can be manipulated far more easily than either the old illiterates, those who could not read, or the genuinely literate. In this way, a minimum reading competency can be seen as an instrument for political control. Therefore, the teaching of literature as a minimum competency— that is, the teaching of appreciation and understanding beyond literal sense—can be justified on the grounds that the very survival of a democracy depends, in part, on the ability of its citizens to interpret events, to see beyond the words on the page to the purposes and intentions of the speaker or writer. Imaginative fiction, because of its shifts in point of view and embedded metaphors, is especially instructive for students in the uses of language.

Writing, too, can be justified on the grounds that through writing students learn to interpret events and documents. That is, writing is both a means of communication and a method of discovery. By trying to write about a subject, one discovers what one knows and believes. But if the minimum competency movement defines the goals of schooling as "job entry skills," then writing, literature, and many other courses may well become identified as financial frills, particularly if the "job entry skills" are defined as being able to write one's name in a blank, remember one's social security number, check "yes" or "no" in response to simple questions, and other so-called survival responses. The minimum competencies define the priorities which determine how money is spent.

Social Effects

The minimum competencies also define the school's gatekeeping function. In this second problem area minimum competencies may determine how students are distributed in the economy and how students are tracked in schools. In Arizona, to receive the standard eighth grade certificate, students are required to be able to read, write, and compute at the sixth grade level of competency. In California, no student shall receive a high school diploma after 1981 who has not passed a minimum competency test. Similar requirements exist in many other states. If in Arizona the eighth grade certificate is required for entrance to ninth grade, the net effect of the California and Arizona statutes is the same: some students will not receive high school diplomas at eighteen and maybe never. Diplomas, like any method of being certified, whether it's to be a lawyer, teacher, or high school graduate, are power. They enable the receiver to apply for and get jobs, to enter other programs for the more advanced certificates which are required for higher paying jobs. To deny a high school diploma is to deny most eighteen year olds the opportunity to enter the mainstream of economic life. And if that eighteen year old without a diploma is black, the labor statistics suggest that he or she has a high probability of being unemployed for some time. Requiring that students pass a minimum competency test in order to get a high school diploma may return schools to the days when they were the absolute gatekeepers to society, sorting students into those who pass and those who fail.

Teachers who find themselves in states where standards of minimum competency will be used to determine who gets a diploma would be well advised to develop those competencies in cooperation with parents and other members of the community. There are a number of ways of involving the community in the definition of minimum competency. Most school districts begin by establishing a proficiency or competency committee which establishes the minimum standards for graduation, often a list of skills like, "Be able to read the newspaper." This committee, composed of both parents and professionals, is asked to suggest how the minimum skills might be measured. This additional step helps define the goals more clearly, moving from "Be able to read the newspaper," to "Be able to read a news story or want ad in the local newspaper."

Next the general community needs to be informed about what the minimum competencies are. In one California community, the language arts coordinator gave the minimum competency test in reading to all tenth graders and members of four community service clubs. (The tenth graders, on the average, did better). Many districts have had sample questions and a self-scoring system printed in local newspapers, providing parents with some idea about what their children are expected to do. Community involvement also had a political purpose—to develop a constituency responsible for the standards and the results. The issuance of diplomas has political consequences, and teachers will need a constituency in the community if the basis for issuing diplomas is not to be characterized as a discrimination by a single professional class.

The tracking of students is another political issue implicit in the gatekeeping function of schools. If students are refused promotion, and stay in school, the public could soon find itself with a rapidly increasing enrollment and a wider range of ages at each grade level. This enrollment increase will require greater funds, and the age ranges may disrupt the social life of the school. Furthermore, if HEW figures are correct, racial and class isolation may be increased. Using evidence from reading tests given to 6,768 youths between 1966 and 1970, HEW has estimated that approximately one million teenagers are seriously deficient in reading and that illiteracy is most prevalent among blacks from low-income families (*Literacy Among Youth 12-17 Years*, Washington, D.C., Government Printing Office, 1973).

If these students who are behind are separated for remedial instruction, then the minimum competency movement could produce an increasing racial and class segregation, even within desegregated schools. If remedial instruction does not mean tracking, then how does a teacher in a heterogeneous class of thirty-five students provide special help for students who are behind? The fact is that the student did not receive adequate help the first time, and there is no reason to believe that special help will be forthcoming the second time in a large, heterogeneous class if class sizes are not reduced or instructional assistants provided. Some remedial instruction programs suggest "alternate management systems within the heterogeneous class." This language may only be an effort to avoid the political controversy inherent in any request for increases in school funding.

Return for a moment to John Mellon's view of what nonreaders need:

> What they *do* need is an hour or more a day alone with an adult, a skillful tutor who can get the right reading material into their hands, deactivate their avoidance and defense mechanisms, praise and encourage every positive attempt they make no matter how badly it miscarries, then "walk alongside them" as they read, nudging them away from attacking *words* and towards daring to inhale whole *sentences*, tolerating regressions and pauses signifying silent re-reading, knowing when to provide a pronunciation or meaning, when to ask for re-reading of a miscue and (more often) when not to, when to choral read, when to have the reader switch from oral to silent or back to oral, when to stop and when to start again, always remembering to affirm, affirm, affirm.

If Mellon's recommendations become typical of remedial instruction, then tracking will not be an issue. But as long as remedial instruction means putting thirty nonreaders together in one class with one teacher, then tracking will become an issue, just as it was in the middle sixties when it was attacked for its segregation of races and sexes. Tracking will only be politically acceptable as long as it has clear educational benefits. Mellon's program has clear educational benefits, but the cost of the program is probably politically unacceptable in some quarters. To get support for higher costs, teachers must make explicit the cost of good educational programs and their social benefits.

Mellon's program is also contrary to the assumptions of most language skills programs which fragment the skills of language into smaller and smaller subdivisions. He believes that the parties responsible for this situation are the giant corporations of education business and "certain college and university educationists who have permitted the concepts of programmed learning, behavioral objectives, and performance criteria to apply to the organization of remedial language skills programs." These educationists, says Mellon, have given publishers "a cloak of respectability with which to conceal the wrongheadedness of their methodology."

The managers of educational bureaucracies, especially the categorical aid programs of federal and state agencies, must share in the responsibility for the fragmenting of language programs. Every categorical aid program requires that a program proposal begin with a needs assessment. Mellon makes the point that "competency testing is unnecessary because the schools know who their non-readers are." So, too, teachers know what the needs are, but in categorical aid programs the only acceptable evidence is test data. So the teachers find some test data. The need is defined by the test, and the test has four parts, which become the four needs: decoding, word attack, vocabulary, and comprehension. Next, the program must fit the needs so, alas, the program has four parts: decoding, word attack, vocabulary, and comprehension. These parts then become the sequence of instruction, and each part has its subunits. For example, word attack has identifying roots, suffixes, and prefixes and separating words into syllables. Comprehension has identifying detail, finding main idea, understanding the difference between fact and opinion, and so forth.

Then the funding arrives, and the students enroll in the program. Odd things begin to happen. First of all, the students who are looking for details are not doing anything different from those looking for main idea. In fact, inferences, ideas, details, facts and opinions all blend. Comprehension is much like seaweed. Pull on one part of it, and the whole blessed thing follows after.

Then, too, there are those students who can read but who are doing decoding because it's the first phase of the program and categorical aid managers love sequence—even though every teacher knows that good readers often put decoding rules last, after all else fails. And then there are those poor students who have to do word attack every day, week after week, because even though they had the highest scores on comprehension, they did poorly on word attack skills.

The whole absurd mess is nicely summarized in a report of the California State Department of Education in which word attack skills were listed as the highest priority for California reading programs and comprehension was listed third. Get that! Being able to attack the word was more important than being able to understand it. The word-bound view of reading ignores the fact that all readers make mistakes. The difference between a good reader and a bad reader is that the good reader corrects the mistakes that matter. In management's view of reading, there is no room for such important reading skills as predicting and guessing. To keep the story line and sense of meaning, students must be encouraged to guess what comes next. Making students word-bound can keep them from remembering what came before, what might come after, thereby rendering the print meaningless. As long as management systems continue to ignore the good sense of teachers and force programs onto a Procrustean bed of standardized tests and sequential instruction, nonsense will continue to fill the pages of minimum competency programs.

Curriculum Decision Making

The minimum competency movement then not only sets goals that determine how schools are funded and how schools track students in and out of schools but also often uses a management system that controls the curriculum through a sequence of behavioral objectives. This is the third problem area—how curriculum decisions are made, especially how nonteachers, those who work in the offices of various educational agencies, attempt to control curriculum. The problem is not new. Raymond Calahan (*Education and the Cult of Efficiency*, University of Chicago Press, 1964), has documented the twentieth century effort to turn the schools into a factory system. And John Dewey complained about the problem seventy-five years ago:

> If there is a single public school in the United States where there is official and constitutional provision made for submitting questions of discipline and teaching to the discussion of those actually engaged in the work of teaching, that fact has escaped my notice.

(John Dewey in *Elementary School Teacher*, quoted by Margaret
Haley in David B. Tyack's *The One Best System*, Harvard University Press, 1974, p. 257)

William Foster's description of how school organizational the-
rists have responded to the lack of confidence in the schools shows
how the minimum competency movement can be seen as part of a
general trend toward centralizing curriculum decisions:

> The response to a crisis in confidence is to attempt to do what
> cannot be done: to objectify even further the ends of administra-
> tion in the hope that these can be made susceptible to technical
> —that is rational—control. ... Applied to the school, the tradi-
> tional legitimacy of the teacher becomes secondary to the means
> of administration. ... Planned curricula development which
> reduces the teacher's autonomy in developing educational aims
> similarly reflects an instrumental rationality whose failure to pro-
> vide a meaningful education may threaten the legitimacy not of
> the academics who develop them but of teachers who are forced
> to use them. ["Administration of the Crisis of Legitimacy: A
> Review of Habermasian Thought." *Harvard Education Review*
> 50 no. 4 (1980): 501]

The minimum competency movement has already produced
numerous mandated programs and step-by-step guides for teaching,
leading to the general institutional view that teachers are routine
workers who carry out the insights from the central office.

Returning Authority to the Classroom Teacher

The key problem here is that K–12 teachers lack the authority they
deserve, authority based on the assumptions that methods and
content in K–12 teaching are a respectable intellectual discipline
and that the intuitions gained from teaching experience are a valuable guide in decision making. Much of what Mellon points to as
good teaching practice has been intuitively identified and developed
by teachers, long before language research was able to validate the
understandings. The area of communicative competence is an
example. Mellon acknowledges that the research in the area is only
beginning and that "It is unclear exactly what forms of classroom
practice may contribute to fuller development of communicative
competence." The classroom possibilities he identifies—role playing, improvisations—have already been intuitively identified and
developed by classroom teachers.

In education today, at the very moment that teachers are seeking power through collective bargaining, teacher authority is at

least as low as it has ever been. There is a difference between power and authority. Power is what is achieved by constituencies—by counting heads and organizing large numbers. The story is told that a lobbying group went to Franklin Delano Roosevelt and gave him an earnest, rational argument supporting their position. He turned to the group and said, "You've convinced me. Now go out and organize some people to make me do it." That's decision by power. Most decisions in education today are legitimized by counting heads and adding up constituencies.

But some important decisions are legitimized by authority, not power, by appeals to expertise in a given area of study, by special knowledge through scholarship. In K-12 teaching, the special knowledge about teaching is granted almost exclusively to those who do not teach K-12 and sometimes have never taught K-12. The leading authorities on teaching practice K-12 are almost never the teachers themselves. Examine the officers and programs of the leading professional associations. Examine the journals on teaching. Examine the references in research on teaching. Examine the dissertations at the leading Schools of Education. In the profession of teaching, the greater one's distance from a classroom, the greater one's pay and authority and the easier one's job.

What can be done to begin to develop an authority for K-12 teachers? First, teachers must begin to do small studies of students learning in classrooms, small case studies of particular types of students. The most appropriate model for teachers is the experience of the medical profession. In the early meetings of the county medical association, doctors would exchange stories on how to treat various injuries and diseases, and later these stories would be summarized and published. When stories agreed on a treatment, a model or theory of treatment was established and accepted until other stories challenged the model. These stories, then, generated a science of medicine.

The second need is model and theory building. As long as every article by a classroom teacher begins as if classroom experiences were idiosyncratic, authority will continue to elude K-12 teachers. Theory building in a profession requires that each article on a problem begin with a review of the relevant literature. In teaching, such a review would have to include unusual genres: unpublished ditto sheet used in tenth grade class at Oakland High School, Ylvisaker, 1973; notes distributed at department meeting, Blickhahn, 1975; and outline used in CATE workshop, Pierce, 1974.

Next, teachers must destroy the myth of teacher-proof materials. Whenever teachers work on guides for the central office, they will insist on a disclaimer at the very beginning: "The contents include some interesting ideas which the teachers on the committee have found useful at one time or another. However, we do not claim they will assist everyone else. We are still a developing profession, as yet without the time and resources to confirm most of the important insights of teachers. We believe that every teacher in this system, facing as he or she does a great variety of teaching challenges, must finally exercise individual, professional judgment on what to teach. This guide cannot be a mandate for a teacher any more than a medical handbook can be a mandate for a doctor. Signed—The Committee."

Organizations like NCTE need to insist that districts begin to use practicing teachers as curriculum consultants, that NIE (National Institute of Education) set aside part of its budget for research on teaching by classroom teachers, that the history of K–12 teachers be researched and honored—in summary that the authority of teachers be developed and recognized. Teachers cannot afford to develop mechanisms for power and ignore mechanisms for authority. If they do, they will end up organizing teachers and find that along the way they have been turned into the watch-dogs of trivia, the monitors of kits and packaged programs, the paper pushers, and form fillers for other people.

If teachers had authority in the profession and, as a result, professional authority within the community, then good teaching practice might survive even the negative pressures of the management systems of the minimum competency movement. In the years ahead, Schools of Education and organizations of teachers should put the professional authority of K–12 teachers as a number one priority.

In the meantime, teachers who participate in the implementation of minimum competency programs should recognize the movement's political implications, decisions on how money is spent, how students are tracked, and how curriculum decisions are made.

Contributors

Charles R. Cooper is Professor, Department of Literature, and Coordinator of Writing Program at the University of California, San Diego. He is coeditor of and contributor to *Evaluating Writing: Describing, Measuring, Judging* (1977) and *Research on Composing: Points of Departure* (1978), coauthor (with J. Jensen and W. Fagan) of *Measures for Research and Curriculum Evaluation* (1975), and the author of *Measuring Growth in Appreciation of Literature* (1972) as well as many journal articles.

Herb Karl is Professor of English Education, University of South Florida. He served as the first multi-media editor of *English Journal* (1973-75) and is a charter member of the NCTE Commission on Media. He has published extensively on media-related subjects in journals such as *The Creative Teacher, Media and Methods,* and *ET CETERA: A Review of General Semantics* and contributed "Electronic Media and the Democratic Vision" to (A. Sampson and V. Baker, eds.) *Proceedings of the 1975 Symposium "L'Entree Deux Guerres."*

John Mellon is Associate Professor of English and Chair of the Program in English Composition, University of Illinois at Chicago Circle. He is the author of the first empirical study of sentence-combining, *Transformational Sentence-Combining,* NCTE Research Report no. 10, (1969) and of a monograph, *National Assessment and the Teaching of English* (1975). Among his other publications are "A Taxonomy of Compositional Competencies" in (R. Beach and P. D. Pearson, eds.) *Perspectives on Literacy* (1978) and "Issues in the Theory and Practice of Sentence-Combining: A Twenty-Year Perspective" in (D. A. Daiker *et al.*, eds.) *Sentence Combining and the Teaching of Writing* (1979).

Miles Myers is Administrative Director of the Bay Area Writing Project, University of California, Berkeley. He has been a high school teacher of English for almost twenty years. He has been Supervisor of Teacher Education at the University of California, Berkeley, and Legislative Advocate for the California Federation of Teachers. He is currently directing a study of the teaching of writing in secondary schools for the National Institute of Education. Among his publications is *A Procedure for Writing Assessment and Holistic Scoring* (1980).

Lee Odell is Professor, Department of Language, Literature, and Communications, Rensselaer Polytechnic Institute. He serves on the Executive Committee and the Publications Committee for *Studies in Rhetoric and Writing* of the Conference on College Composition and Communication. He is coeditor of and contributor to *Evaluating Writing: Describing, Measuring, Judging* (1977) and *Research on Composing: Points of Departure* (1978). His three-year study (with Dixie Goswami) of writing in nonacademic settings, funded by the National Institute of Education, is nearly completed.

Alan Purves is Director of Curriculum Laboratory and Professor of English Education, University of Illinois at Urbana-Champaign. He is also Past President of NCTE. His publications include (with R. Beach) *Literature and the Reader* (1972), *Literature Education in Ten Countries* (1973), *Achievement in Reading and Literature in the Secondary Schools: New Zealand in International Perspective* (1979), *Reading and Literature: American Achievement in International Perspective* (1981), and other books and articles.